Praise for
Merchants of Enterprise
Private Equity in Canada: The Colour and Controversy

"The definitive Canadian resource on everything private equity did, does and will do. A must-read before you invest dollar one in any private equity deal."

Kevin O'Leary
Chairman O'Leary Funds
TV Co-host on CBC's Lang/O'Leary Exchange, Dragon's Den and ABC'S Shark Tank

"Miriam Varadi understands private equity in Canada and she has laid it out clearly and intelligently for everyone interested in this important part of our financial marketplace. If you are interested in private equity this is a 'must-read'."

Gerald W. Schwartz
Chairman and CEO
Onex Corporation

"Miriam takes a relatively unknown industry and through a series of detailed interviews, simplifies it to make it understandable to the reader. I believe it is a Canadian first and well worth the read."

Brent Belzberg
Senior Managing Partner
TorQuest Partners Inc.

"Having become the first author to chronicle the history and progression of Canadian private equity, Varadi has immediately vaulted herself to become the authority on the subject. Her natural story-telling ability combines elegantly with the expertise of a sophisticated investment executive. The result is a highly informative and enjoyable treatise on Canadian private equity that reads like a cross between a Josh Lerner textbook and a Peter C. Newman page turner. Bravo Miriam!"

Bruce M. Rothney
Deputy Chairman
RBC Capital Markets

"In *Merchants of Enterprise*, Miriam Varadi brings much needed clarity and accessibility to the opportunities and challenges of the private equity market in Canada. For business students and investors considering broadening their investment portfolio, *Merchants of Enterprise* is a helpful resource that delivers straight-forward insight and knowledge. I particularly applaud Miriam's informal and easy-to-read format, enlivened with personal experiences and conversations that help shine a light of understanding on this important financial market, even as it continues to evolve."

Carol Stephenson
Lawrence G. Tapp Chair in Leadership
Dean of the Richard Ivey School of Business,
University of Western Ontario

Merchants of Enterprise
Private Equity in Canada:
The Colour and Controversy

FidRisk
C O L L E C T I O N

Merchants of Enterprise
Private Equity in Canada:
The Colour and Controversy

Miriam Varadi

CARSWELL®

Bibliothèque et Archives nationales du Québec and Library and Archives Canada cataloguing in publication

Varadi, Miriam, 1947-

    Merchants of enterprise: private equity in Canada: the colour and controversy

    (Collection FidRisk; 2)
    Includes bibliographical references and index.

    ISBN 978-0-7798-1940-9

    1. Private equity - Canada. 2. Investments - Canada. 3. Private equity. I. Title. II. Series: FidRisk collection; 2.

HG4751.V37 2009   332.60971   C2009-942583-1

THOMSON REUTERS

CARSWELL, A DIVISION OF THOMSON REUTERS CANADA LIMITED

One Corporate Plaza	Customer Relations
2075 Kennedy Road	Toronto 1-416-609-3800
Toronto, Ontario	Elsewhere in Canada/U.S. 1-800-387-5164
M1T 3V4	Fax 1-416-298-5082
	www.carswell.com
	E-mail www.carswell.com/email

To my son, Benjamin Leon Varadi, whose private equity strategy is to invest in the hopes and dreams of his friends. This book is written to broaden his horizon and reveal Canada's wealth of opportunities in this expanding field.

CONTENTS

PART I
THE BACKGROUND

INVESTMENT ALTERNATIVES

My interest in private equity starts from the vantage point of public stock markets; the lessons learned and the experience gathered. In 2005, I was struck by a sudden and severe illness. As I lay there feeling wretched, my mind spinning, I reflected on the fact that I had been an observer of one of the most innovative periods in financial history. After an active 27-year career, I focused on the significance of my experience in public markets in order to explore new trends, especially in the rapidly growing field of private equity.

As I looked back, my mind rested on a historic moment, the fall of the Berlin Wall in 1989. While the world focused on the political meaning, to those in the financial world it signaled the triumph of Western-style public stock markets.

Economically, government central planning had failed in favour of the instant feedback system of Western stock markets. Communist countries from China to Russia scrambled to implement their own version of these free markets.

Most of us in the investment industry reveled in our victory and self-importance, but a new competitor focused on the flaws in public stock markets: a new paradigm of private equity was evolving. To put this in perspective, I needed to understand the chain of events through my personal recollections.

When I started my career during the 1970s, Canadians' wealth lay in the value of their home or their business. They slept soundly with high interest rate certificates at their local banks. If they were really lucky, they had an RRSP or a company pension plan. Market information was rare and most people had never even heard the word 't-bill'.

1

By the 1990s all that had changed. Huge numbers of people were seriously experiencing the market for the first time due to the changed financial environment. Traditional jobs and businesses were disappearing as were dependable pensions. Interest rates had dropped dramatically and so had the value of people's homes. Almost everyone needed financial planning help. Stock market information exploded; TV and radio stations with minuteby-minute financial information flooded the airwaves. I laughed when a beleaguered 'real estate' industry advertised in the late 1990s that you can't live in a mutual fund. The irony!

As I built my practice I watched public stock markets grow in sophistication and innovation. At the end of the 20th century, many thought the best growth industry of the previous 25 years was high tech. It was not. The best growth was in the financial industry. New vehicles such as hedge funds, futures and derivatives made my hair frizz. Money was on steroids. People had developed ways of making the same dollar go a thousand ways further and change hands a thousand times faster. No dream was too big to finance. There was money to fund a high tech revolution, billion dollar rock stars and heady emerging markets. If the dream was inspiring enough, the money followed like an eager puppy.

I learned the immense power of our world to create wealth. It taught me that money is simply the handmaiden of our collective goals and desires. It gave me faith in open but regulated financial markets and a profound belief in the financial industry to fuel ideas, achievements and aspirations, no matter how big or daunting.

I saw the end of a world of the privileged few where all investments were local. The corridors of power had grown and expanded worldwide. Gone were the days when a handful of privileged investors could treat public markets like a private club and profit with impunity. Once share ownership became widespread, there were many watching eyes and punishments began to fit the crimes.

Sadly, investors are currently focused on the recession and the problems in the financial sector. Like all human endeavour, markets are subject to greed and excess. When anything expands too quickly the corrections are equally forceful. The amazing phenomenon of a market economy has been the ability of open markets to self-cleanse and repair system failures. My life's work has been to follow the thread of evolving opportunity.

Having spent my life helping people build investment portfolios, the quest for profitable investments was second nature to me and I wanted to understand and find new opportunities. I felt that I could use my experience in public equities to gain insights into private equity. My goal was personal growth and the desire to mentor a new generation.

When I built my career in the financial industry and carved my niche, I felt public markets were at the epicenter of the action. After 2005, as I gazed out from the vantage point of experience, I observed the rapid expansion of a new and growing breed of private equity professionals, functioning as active shareholders and playing key roles in management and growth of their portfolio businesses. In light of the meltdown, the financial press often alluded to private equity's role in the crisis and in its solution. New concepts like 'Private Equity Fund', 'Fund of Funds' and 'General Partner' were used by journalists without sufficient background.

Prior to 2005, I vaguely followed the private equity scene from afar. There was a growing awareness of private equity and its increasing role, but I mistrusted it and wondered why it was gaining ground. As I researched private equity for this book, I tested my assumptions by interviewing the individuals directly involved. Sometimes, this resulted in lively conversations as I expressed my doubts and pressed professionals for their convictions. I went armed with a core list of questions:

- Why is private equity gaining ground?
- Where does Canada stand in this new field?
- Is private equity a worthwhile investment choice and what are the new rules of the game?
- Does it outperform public stocks?
- What are the risks and rewards?
- Who are the suitable investors?
- Who are the participants and how does one gain entry into this realm?
- Does it have a future?

This book aims to answer these questions. Parts I and II of this book invite you into the world of private equity. They introduce the concepts, acquaint you with the jargon and share the rules of engagement. I set the stage by describing the need for private equity, its phenomenal growth and the struggle that led to its success. However, it is only the beginning. I give you the information you need to enter this world; a sense of how things work.

3

In Part III, I change pace and share the wisdom of several practitioners. During extensive conversations, each one of these professionals generously offers the understanding that comes with experience. Hopefully, you will be intrigued by the colour of private equity.

In Part IV, 'The Controversy', the pace increases, taking you behind the scenes and allowing you to grapple with the issues, mistakes and problems of this nascent industry. As in public stock markets, the meltdown has exposed its warts.

The book would be incomplete without a glimpse of the future. Having explored this question with professionals in the field, I end with my impression of how private equity will evolve and move forward.

Finally, as a bonus, for those Canadians who would like to pursue private equity further, there is a tax and legal chapter written by two experts, one from a premier Canadian accounting firm and another from a leading legal firm.

For well over a year now, I have been embedded in the private equity world. I have met a fascinating new cast of characters and learned the rules of the industry. This book is written to share my experience. I hope you enjoy the journey as much as I did.

CONTRASTING PRIVATE AND PUBLIC EQUITY

*"When quoted stock prices no longer dominate
decision-making, the rules of the game change."*

Andrew Brenton, CEO,
Turtle Creek Asset Management Inc.

Private equity and public equity are both actors on the same stage; sometimes uniting, other times parting ways. Although most investors are schooled in public markets, there is a growing awareness of private markets and an interest in how they function.

In recent years, the public has been mesmerized by a spotlight cast on high profile private equity firms (PE firms) such as KKR, Blackstone and the Carlyle Group. Investors who tracked their rise were awed by their vast fortunes, deal-making prowess and increasing power. This has piqued curiosity about private equity, though most remain mystified by the inner workings of this illusive investment style.

This is surprising considering its growth and importance. At the end of 2007, financing through PE firms had increased 50-fold over 20 years and represented a value of $2.5 trillion.[1] During most of that time, the industry grew gradually, but exploded between 2000-2006 when the sector's total assets jumped by 120%.[2] This is certainly a force to be reckoned with but it remains largely unexamined by the general public. Most individuals feel they have no stake in private equity and most investors follow only public equity markets.

In fact, private equity has become mainstream and impacts more lives than is generally known. The goal of this book is to explain how private equity works and its opportunities. Individual investors will be able to take advantage of private equity once they are aware of their choices.

Large pension plans in both Canada and the U.S., have substantial private equity holdings. Therefore, a significant number of employees will see their pension performance affected by private equity returns. Of greater significance is the number of household names such as Shoppers Drug Mart, Laura Secord, Yellow Pages, Celestica and Sleep Country Canada that were (or are still) owned by private equity firms. So the question arises as to how

---

1. David Rubenstein, co-founder of the Carlyle Group, "The Rise and Rise of Private Equity", *The Economist, The World in 2008*, December, 2007.
2. *The Economist*, March 1, 2008.

the business practices of major private equity firms impact not only the investors but the welfare of employees, management, customers, suppliers and their communities.

As we learned from the 2008 financial meltdown, we are more connected to the investment world than we realize. Its activities impact our daily lives, jobs and lifestyles. As taxpayers, we often have to pay for their errors of judgment and regulatory failures.

This section aims to explain private equity's rapid growth and the reasons behind it. I start my story in 1979 in the area where my career began, public stock markets when private equity was a little known experiment.

In 1979, I was in the right place at the right time. Stock markets were ready to stage a significant comeback after a long stretch with disappointing performance. From 1973 to 1975, North American economies had suffered a deep and prolonged recession and faith in stock markets was not yet restored. The last long-term investors were throwing in the towel, swearing off the stock market forever. Brokerage houses were awash with tales of woe and cynical market commentaries abounded. In contrast, the next 25 years were to produce one of the most lucrative and creative periods in stock market history.

Although I agonized through my share of market ups and downs, during the rest of my career there was a steadily climbing trajectory as the Dow climbed from 901.32 in August of 1982 to 10,173 by August of 2004. To mention a few of the highlights: an extended period of falling interest rates, the "democratization of wealth", the high tech revolution, globalization and the zenith of the power and influence of North American financial institutions.

But in 1979, when clients asked me about private investing, I would look dumbfounded. At that time, private investment meant direct investing. In other words, buying and managing a business or becoming a silent partner in someone else's business. "Why bother?" I thought. Public markets were so much more prestigious, reliable and trustworthy. Private investments were for those investors who wanted to roll up their sleeves, do their own due diligence, get involved in on-going supervision and take excessive risks for dubious returns. Perhaps that was required if you had no other means of building a nest-egg, but for anyone with spare funds, public markets offered a better chance of wealth preservation.

Enthusiastically, I recited the pluses of public investing. There is the issue of liquidity: when you open the newspaper in the morning you know what your investment can fetch. You buy and sell with confidence based on an auction system that is there to serve you. If you need to sell large or small positions to maintain your lifestyle, for estate planning or any emergency, then public markets facilitate those actions.

A successful business owner could take a company public in order to cash out or retire. The stock market offers a seller better liquidity, generally higher valuations and an army of advisors and traders ready to help an owner on his way. Meanwhile, the next generation can grow their wealth by buying shares in listed companies and accumulating stock as their income grows. Because up and coming individuals lack the capital to buy valuable businesses, this is an important way to transition ownership gradually.

Alternatively, successful business owners, who go public with the objective of growing their business, find raising capital through public markets more efficient. They can by-pass overly cautious bankers and find accommodating investment dealers who receive a fee for transferring risk to third parties. When a stock is publicly traded, companies are easier to appraise; so investment dealers can sell its bonds and debentures to finance future growth.

Employees could take comfort in the bosom of a public company since employment there was considered more secure. In addition, ready-made incentive systems through stock options were a tempting bonus to offer executives, and gave listed companies a hiring advantage over private rivals. That was an age of innocence, when the cost of options was not revealed in annual financial statements and therefore hidden from scrutiny. It was win-win for the company and management.

For investors, public markets have significant advantages. All financial information is available to everyone at the same time. Hence, there is more transparency and insider trading is strictly forbidden. Most important, markets are regulated by government for investor protection, which offers more enforceable governance.

In the grand scheme of things, there is a cachet to customers, suppliers, founders, employees and investors being involved with listed companies. These all-stars have passed the rigours of listing on a public stock market and have successfully maintained their status. There is pride and prestige that comes with being listed.

The Fall from Grace of Public Stock Markets

It is hard to know when the tables turned and whether the recent fall from grace of public markets is just a temporary phase, a resting stop after a heady period of over two decades.

What caused the fall? Many things conspired around the turn of the millennium.

There was the dotcom bubble and disenchantment with the way many analysts, investment bankers and investment advisors behaved in less than honourable ways. It certainly shed an unflattering light on how public markets can be manipulated.

There was Enron and a host of dishonest listed companies that shamelessly and flagrantly violated public trust. Perhaps option mispricing helped, revealing huge potential costs which were not clearly disclosed in financial reports. In addition, there were those over-paid executives in companies that failed to turn a profit.

The abuse brought down the heavy hand of U.S. regulators who imposed the *Sarbanes-Oxley* regulations causing outcries against onerous regulations. Would future CEOs become paper-pushing bureaucrats? These things all led to a re-examination of listed public markets.

However, public markets still offer the same benefits as before:

1. Liquidity: the ease of buying and selling in a well-developed auction system. Shares may be over-valued or under-valued; you may be delighted with the price you receive or disappointed. Nevertheless, there is always access to the market and a place to deal for a portion or a whole position.

2. Transition: the ability to attract talent and shift opportunity from one generation to the next is easier when shares are constantly traded. The up-and-coming buy shares when they can afford them and sell when they need to raise cash.

3. Options: the ability to offer incentives by using stock options is still an excellent way to encourage people. It offers a fair and easy way for hard-working employees to evaluate their rewards. Being able to open a newspaper each day and calculate the value of your bonus is a great motivator.

4. Transparency and Governance: There are rules and regulations for reporting timely financial information and material changes in a company. All the information must be available to all shareholders at the same time to create a fair and open market. In addition there are regulators to enforce the rules. There is someone to watch over you.

For the bulk of investable assets, stock markets will always hold the upper hand. Institutions such as pension funds, insurance companies and mutual funds need the instant access of this marketplace for a significant portion of their assets. Since they deal in other people's money, they require the liquidity, transparency and regulation mandated in the public domain. Individual investors building a nest egg also need the protection of the stock market.

The flexibility and efficiency of stock markets is unbeatable. Nevertheless, beneath the surface, throughout my career, I observed a growing chasm between shareholders and management who ran public companies. As stock markets flourished, share ownership became more widespread and dispersed among ever greater numbers. As a result, the influence of shareholders over key decisions waned. Pension funds and institutions in search of healthy returns questioned the motives of management in listed public companies.

At the helm of listed companies, executives and their boards were united in their common interest and in mutual support. Therefore, they had control over key decisions. Powerful institutions, such as pension funds, questioned whether executives and boards were acting in the best interests of investors (who provided capital) or were inhibited by their mutual vested interest, need for safety and the status quo. In other words, were executives and boards acting as caretakers without adding sufficient value? Major shareholders wanted a way to influence business decisions to focus on growth and profits. There was growing dissatisfaction and an under-current for change.

The first public shockwave hit in 1988 when KKR, a private equity group subsequently described as the 'Barbarians at The Gate',[3] snapped up stodgy RJR Nabisco, in 1988, converting it from a public to a private company. This seminal event signaled a new direction in investment management. In fact, from the 1970s onward, a few professional investors, determined to reassert their influence as owners, had quietly started to purchase inefficiently run listed companies and take them private in order to maximize their value. Often this

---

3. Bryan Burrough and John Helyar, *Barbarians at the Gate: The Fall of RJR Nabisco* (New York: Harper & Row, 1990).

involved the break-up of the company. This started as an unproven, inconsistent investment technique and Nabisco represented the first public awareness of the change. Gradually, a new model of private equity evolved and became a large global industry.

Prior to the 1970s, private equity was hamstrung by limited options for raising money. Private financiers were at the mercy of banks and bankers who held a despotic hold over their funding. Since banks and bankers were advancing their own money and would be held accountable for any failures, they exercised extreme caution. They were the gatekeepers who could make or break a private deal.

Talk to any businessman about bankers and there is universal angst. One entrepreneur described banks as "institutions that lend you an umbrella when the sun is shining but take it away at the first sign of clouds."

Starting in the 1970s, capital markets developed more accommodating methods for participating in the private arena which allowed institutions like pension funds, insurance companies and endowments to replace over-cautious banks as providers of capital to PE firms.

The most controversial new entrants to investing in private equity are the "sovereign wealth funds". As the name implies, these are large pools of capital that belong to a national government. One well-publicized transaction in May, 2007 was the large purchase of shares by the Government of China in Blackstone, one of the largest PE firms in the U.S.

While failings in corporate governance in public equity helped create the new dynamics of private equity, the growing sophistication of private equity funding and better access to private opportunities also led to its growth. Now, in addition to public stocks and bonds, private equity has joined the ranks of acceptable asset classes and is included in a category called alternative investments.

Private investing can be done through private equity funds, mutual funds and closed-end funds. These are ways of repackaging private investments into digestible amounts for investors. The three main alternative investments are private equity, real estate and hedge funds. Here we deal only with private equity.

Profitable Points

(Contrasting Private and Public Equity)

- *The success of private equity has piqued investors' curiosity although most still know little about this investment alternative. Therefore, they do not know how to participate. The goal of this book is to explain how private equity works and its opportunities.*

- *Over the past decade, private equity has become mainstream and impacts more people than ever before. This is because public pension plans and major financial institutions have made sizeable commitments to this growing asset class. Also, many Canadians are now employed in businesses owned by private equity interests.*

- *The growth of private equity resulted from powerful individuals and institutions searching for better returns and questioning the governance of some publicly listed companies.*

- *Despite the focus on the shortcomings of listed companies, stock markets have advantages over private equity, such as liquidity, transparency and better governance.*

- *In the past, private equity was hamstrung because of its dependency on banks for financing. Since the 1970s this has changed as other capital providers, such as pension funds, replaced the banks. The rise of private equity resulted from this better access to financing.*

- *Private equity is now included in investment portfolios in the category called alternative assets along with real estate and hedge funds.*

THE ASCENT OF PRIVATE EQUITY

*"Creativity is thinking up new things. Innovation is
doing new things."*

Theodore Levitt, an American Economist,
Canadian Business, Capital Ideas, March 16, 2009

The Nature of Private Equity

At its simplest, the term 'private equity' refers to ownership of companies that are not listed on a stock exchange; in other words, private companies. For these companies, there is no central market to determine their value. Contrast this with public companies, whose ownership is shared among holders of the company's stock. The stock is traded in open markets and so the price of the stock (and, by extension, the value of the company) is always clear. Moreover, stock prices are constantly re-appraised based on up-to-date economic and financial data.

In the case of public companies, countless investors buy and sell shares every day, reflecting their differing views of the companies' prospects. In the case of private companies, the number of people willing to invest their money is much smaller, as there is no market-set price, less information, less regulation and no certainty that you will be able to sell your shares quickly if needed. Often there is only one bidder in private equity investments and never more than a handful. For an informed professional buyer, there is always the possibility of snapping up a company at a great discount; the unguarded "Honey Pot". On the other hand, an uninformed buyer can be grossly misled. There is an old French proverb, "There are more fools among buyers than among sellers".

Since it is difficult to buy and sell, private equity investments tend to be for the long-term. As one wag quipped, most private equity investments last longer than the average marriage. Once you sign the legal documents, you are in for a long-term commitment, up to ten years, with no easy out.

In addition, private equity investments generally offer limited cash flow, with the pay off coming at the end (when investments are sold or closed out) so investors only know in hindsight if the effort was rewarding. The lack of liquidity hurts both investors and business owners. The benefit of selling shares in a business piecemeal at an owner's convenience, as in public markets, should never be underestimated.

In view of the disadvantages, what types of businesses would opt to be sold privately? There are two broad categories of private equity investments: venture and buyouts. Venture refers to small companies, often start-ups, which do not qualify for listing on a public market and would not generally be able to afford the costs even if they did. In contrast, the second category, buyouts, are larger, established, and more mature businesses. These are revenue-generating companies.

Businesses that are categorized as buyouts might qualify for listing on a stock exchange, but the business owners may have reasons for maintaining a veil of secrecy. When an established business is up for a public sale it creates uncertainty about the future; key employees could leave, suppliers might abandon them and competitors could target the sellers' clients for their own benefit.

For personal reasons, owners might prefer a private sale. Wealthy sellers (especially in smaller communities) might not want their neighbours made aware of their net worth, so they avoid the disclosure of public markets. Even governments occasionally desire secrecy when selling politically sensitive assets.

In the U.K., during the Thatcher era, the railways were quickly and quietly sold in a series of private equity transactions to avoid publicity. The buyout firms involved made a handsome profit and this historic operation has been dubbed "The Great Train Robbery".

Overall, the advantages of private equity seemed overwhelming during the liquidity boom of 2006 when stock markets took a back seat, hampered by intrusive media coverage, the tedium of bureaucratic corporate governance codes, activist investors, short sellers and the polemics of self-serving politicians. Operating in the public eye involves more regulation, scrutiny and less control for the business owner. In that one year the private equity industry worldwide raised a record $459 billion.

However, the steady growth began in the late 1980s as financial markets evolved and the drawbacks of private equity became less onerous, particularly raising capital. The investment industry became adept at freeing capital, moving it quickly and making it work harder. This was referred to as financial engineering and resulted in the creation of new types of financing vehicles, such as hedge funds and structured products. Such offshoots became big sources of funding and gradually displaced the ever-cautious banks.[4]

---

4. "The Business of Making Money, Briefing Public v. Private Equity", *The Economist*, July 7th, 2007.

This increase in capital, coupled with a general discontent that major investors were experiencing in listed markets, fueled the growth of a new discipline. Powerful individuals and institutions searching for better returns and questioning mismanagement of some listed companies were attracted to the idea of making direct investments in private companies instead, but were reluctant to do it on their own. Instead, they increasingly backed the newly formed private equity firms (PE firms) that had the expertise in evaluating and governing private companies, but needed large injections of capital to build up their portfolios of companies.

As this private equity model gained experience and credibility, it began to cast a negative shadow on the public equity model. Being on exhibit at all times and experiencing greater regulation created a double edged sword. Although stock markets are more transparent and efficient, being public creates a great deal of distraction and increased obstacles. Private markets in addition to their privacy offer advantages which will become increasingly evident as we proceed.

Profitable Points

(The Ascent of Private Equity)

- *Private businesses are harder to evaluate than publicly traded companies, which makes them both more difficult to finance and harder to buy and sell.*

- *An important caveat to remember is that private equity lacks liquidity; as a result, investments tend to be for the long-term (up to 10 years).*

- *With the help of financial engineering, more money became available in the closing years of the 20th century, making it easier for PE firms to do deals. There are now many new ways for private companies to obtain financing.*

- *PE firms developed in order to evaluate and oversee private businesses for investors, such as institutions and wealthy individuals.*

- *Being shielded from public scrutiny gives private equity a strategic advantage: It is less obstructed by outside influences such as the media, polemics and corporate governance codes.*

14

PART II
THE BASICS

SECTION I: THE PURSUIT

ANATOMY OF A PE FIRM

"Private Equity firms build to the trend. First they look at the industry, envision the future, and then they must transform their portfolio companies into industry leaders."

Doug McDonald, Partner,
Financial Advisory Private Company Services,
Deloitte & Touche LLP

World's Oldest Investment

When I told people that I was writing a book about private equity, they looked at me reassuredly as though the meaning was obvious, but if I asked what they knew about private equity, they seemed perplexed. This is because private equity has been revitalized. The change spawned an industry and created a fresh perspective.

Private equity has always existed; it is the oldest way to invest in business. Until the industrial revolution most businesses were relatively small with limited requirements and privately owned by the people who operated them.

The Industrial Revolution changed the face of business; businesses needed additional capital to build factories and manufacture equipment. Financial markets evolved as the demand for capital increased. More and more investors pooled their resources to provide sufficient capital to build and run the new economy. These investor syndicates were eventually organized into stock markets and as these markets grew, ownership was dispersed among ever larger numbers of public shareholders who were not actively involved in the operations of the business.

15

This widespread ownership made it hard to effect change in a poorly managed business. The executives and board of directors that ran these corporations often lacked the will to make tough decisions. They were reluctant to sell underperforming assets, close unprofitable divisions, or return money to shareholders. Instead, they diversified into businesses where they lacked expertise and often failed. BCE, a telephone company in Canada, once bought a trust company, and I remember thinking what an absurd combination. Corporate governance deteriorated throughout the twentieth century as a wealthier growing middle class piled into public stock markets, further widening the gap between shareholders and business management.

Shareholders were perceived as passive, and some company leaders became less rigorous in promoting shareholders' interests. When I worked in public markets, there were attempts to rectify this problem. At first, there was a proliferation of activist shareholders. However, activist shareholders lacked control. They could complain all they wanted, but couldn't fire bad management. They did not have the power to create change or fix problems.

Beginning in the1960s, in the U.S., there was a series of private equity transactions which involved various investors who bought the entire share capital of public companies and reorganized them to create more valuable businesses. It was part of a move towards hands-on management and more direct ownership. The new investors wanted control and a results-oriented approach to business decisions. These investors needed organizations that would work with them to meet these goals. This ultimately resulted in the creation of PE firms. Generally, a PE firm in its present form consists of a group of professionals who finance and oversee a handful of businesses in which these professionals have a personal stake.

Owning Up

The role of a PE firm is to fund businesses. As part of the process they identify attractive businesses, negotiate the purchase, grow them and finally negotiate their sale. Because these firms are a reaction to deficiencies in stock markets, they are structured to avoid similar drawbacks. The purpose of a PE firm is to assume the responsibility of ownership and add value to the businesses under their care. Although they rarely manage the business, they do oversee operations and are compensated based on successful outcomes.

There are many models of PE firms. Our exemplary firm is independent and owned by its partners. Like most PE firms it is small compared to similar professional firms such as accounting or legal firms. This is because much of the work is hands-on, so senior people can't delegate easily to their subordinates. Private equity professionals have an investment or business background and usually come from investment banking or accounting firms. Partners are seasoned professionals and are responsible for approving and reviewing all business commitments.

On average there is one junior professional to support every senior partner; a generous ratio is two juniors per partner. Whereas juniors research and analyze both industries and companies, partners make the critical decisions. The juniors all have professional designations but insufficient industry experience. It takes years of apprenticeship to learn the skills of a partner. Together, partners and juniors review and monitor their businesses on an on-going basis. They develop business strategies, hire executives, engage an independent board, and allocate capital so that the business grows.

This is a labour-intensive activity so the maximum number of businesses the average PE firm can manage at one time is about ten. Most PE firms want control and majority ownership in each business. Occasionally they take a minority position, which involves less work, and then they can manage more businesses at a given time.

In fulfilling their role, their first responsibility is fund raising from inactive investors who are not involved in on-going business decisions. To attract capital and gain the support of sophisticated backers, PE firms must convince them that both the firm and its inactive investors are pursuing a collective goal and have similar interests. The active partners who both manage the capital and offer advice and support to each business are known as the general partners (GPs). Inactive investors supplying only capital are called limited partners (LPs). The cornerstone of the relationship between PE firms and inactive investors is referred to as an 'alignment of interests'.

Sharing the Risks

In PE firms the 'alignment of interests' starts with the professional compensation. When a firm is raising money for a portfolio of businesses (called a fund), the firm normally receives an annual fee of 2% of the committed capital. This percentage covers the firm's expenses and compensates the professionals. The compensation is not designed to be generous and most partners could earn more elsewhere.

Savvy investors look at a PE firm's budget to ensure that the percentage is in line with cost expectations or else they renegotiate for a lower percentage.

These firms are run by working partners and this 2% covers their costs and income, but is not the main source of their profit.

In addition, partners are expected to commit their own capital to the fund. Consequently the PE firm as a whole has a significant capital commitment in every fund. In a given fund, the capital risk of inactive investors and active partners should be comparable; if inactive investors lose, so do the active partners. This is where the rubber hits the road, when both active partners and inactive investors share the downside risk. Also, partners must invest on the same terms and conditions as inactive partners.

Readers may now wonder why anyone would want the responsibility of an active partner. The reward comes later, based on success. PE firms receive a substantial share of the profits (normally 20%) after investors have received their initial capital back. This percentage of profits is called the 'carry'. After approximately ten years, when a profitable fund is closed out, the PE firm will have received 20% of all the profits and the inactive investors receive 80% of the profits.

In public markets, management sometimes makes acquisitions or finances projects that do not serve the shareholders' best interests despite the fact that the company's board of directors is intended to represent the shareholders. In private equity, the responsibility of a PE firm is to safeguard against such fruitless undertakings by allocating capital more efficiently. To achieve this they assess strategy, risk and opportunity to optimize success for its LPs. Because the GPs' own capital is at risk, the assumption is that the PE firms' approach will be more cautious and disciplined than that of some public company boards. There is said to be a clearer alignment of mutual interests between GPs and LPs than in the case of boards of many public corporations and its shareholders.

It is very difficult for any PE firm to raise money for its first fund. Investors want to see a track record that is consistent, understandable and repeatable. They want reassurance that their money will be invested wisely. The goal of private equity is to tie the firm's partners into a fund and create a reliable team that remains in place throughout the life of the fund. This serves to produce a consistent result and is accomplished by requiring partners to invest their personal cash alongside their investors. Ultimately, it aligns the professionals with the business strategy in order to duplicate previous successful track records.

Many experts argue that these new PE firms create a better model for managing businesses, because GPs and LPs have comparable risks. As a result, these experts believe that businesses owned and managed by a PE firm deploy capital more efficiently and have better managed balance sheets. In addition, PE firms provide better oversight so decisions in the businesses owned by them are more strategic.

Profitable Points

(Anatomy of a PE Firm)

- *Public shareholders cannot easily present a unified front and therefore it is hard to change a poorly managed company. PE firms evolved as a movement towards better management in private businesses and hence improved profitability.*

- *The role of a PE firm is to finance businesses. As part of the process, it selects businesses, negotiates the purchase, grows them and finally negotiates a sale.*

- *Most PE firms handle fewer than ten businesses at any one time.*

- *To attract capital and avoid the pitfalls of listed companies, the interests of GPs and LPs must be aligned.*

- *To align investors' interests, most PE firms make a significant capital commitment to the funds that they manage and therefore they share the same downside risks as their inactive investors.*

- *PE firms are in charge of allocating capital efficiently to their various businesses. Because their own money is at risk, it is assumed that partners will take a deliberate and focused approach to spending investors' money.*

- *It is very difficult for any PE firm to raise capital for its first fund because investors want to see a successful, consistent and repeatable track record.*

THE GO-BETWEENS: MERGER & ACQUISITION (M&A) FIRMS

The sale of a private business is usually an emotionally charged process. It represents far more than a dollar figure. The lives of the entrepreneur and his family are wrapped up in the business. Entrepreneurs are not known for their balanced life styles and most speak of the sacrifice and dedication required to build a business. The buyers' needs can also be complex. Typically, the sellers are the owners who built the business and a PE firm is the purchaser.

Intermediaries or go-betweens are usually needed to add a rationale and restore calm to the sales process. They are hired by, and represent, the vendor. The two main players are the merger and acquisition (M&A) firms and the consultants. Neither intermediary buys or funds businesses. This allows them to be objective when dealing with business owners. Their role is to enhance the value of a business and smooth its transfer. They act as mediators between a seller and a buyer. M&A firms and consultants are also used by listed companies and to help a business grow instead of being sold.

M&A Firms: The Agents

M&A firms act as agents. Their role is to sell a business and their compensation is based on the closing price. However, unlike the typical agent who sells but is not qualified to advise, the individuals in M&A are trained professionals with legal, accounting, or financial designations. Deals are in danger of not closing if a business is not properly advised and prepared for sale. When I used the word 'agent' in conversation with a partner at an M&A firm, he frowned. M&A professionals see themselves as 'advisors' rather than agents and distinguish themselves by their levels of service. They believe the advice comes first and the sale second.

There is a plethora of mid-sized firms with varying professional capabilities that perform M&A services. Their professionals inspect all aspects of the business: management, accounting, legal systems and acquire a thorough understanding of how the business functions. Then they can recommend appropriate actions. M&A divisions also exist within accounting firms and at investment dealers. Occasionally, PE firms hire M&A specialists to help them sell a business.

M&A firms put the business in order so that it can be well presented; they quarterback the sales process and make sure that the business can withstand a thorough due diligence. They are there to ensure that the deal will close.

Selling a business is not their only role. M&A specialists are driven by projects. Business owners approach them when there is an event. The sale of a business is one of the major triggers. Other important M&A functions occur when owners want to expand, prepare for succession planning or reduce their risk: perhaps 100% of the owners' money is tied up in the business and they feel too vulnerable.

One professional I interviewed said it is not uncommon to have several goals at once. He had an important client trying to accomplish three of the four objectives at the same time. The owner wanted to take some money out to reduce his personal risk, grow the business from $50 million to $150 million by buying his competitor and do some succession planning so he could work less. The M&A firm met all the client's objectives. Unlike a PE firm, an M&A firm has no conflict of interest because it is not buying the business.

The most common method for an M&A firm to sell a business is by arranging a business auction. These are specialized silent auctions where buyers are invited to bid after going through a vetting process. Such screened auctions are carefully orchestrated to maintain the confidentiality of the seller. The advantage of auctions is that owners stand the chance of receiving the best price. If the business is sold, the M&A firm is paid a commission based on the sale price.

Consulting Firms: The Planners

Consulting firms serve a different function; they analyze and advise on particular problems within a business. Consultants are experts in a specific field and have a wide knowledge of their area. There are now a multitude of consulting firms with different niches.

For example, there are consultants that assess the position of a business within its industry; they study the competition, customers and overall industry in order to determine their client's competitive advantage. There are operational consultants that analyze how efficiently an individual business is functioning independent of the competition; the biggest business challenges are cutting costs, increasing profits or growing.

In a society where lawsuits are more common, consultants can provide due diligence assessments tailored to business requirements, such as legal, accounting or environmental issues. A consultant targets the owners' need, analyzes the problem and designs a solution. Consulting firms can be generalists and work with different types of goals or some specialize in defined areas.

A consultant does strategic work of on-going importance to a business whereas M&A professionals are deal brokers. Consultants work with a business to evaluate the viability of a project. Often there is no immediate change on the horizon and instead they are instrumental in business planning. In contrast, M&A firms are motivated by transitions, such as a sale, restructuring or financing of a business. Like M&A firms, consultants also work for PE firms during business deals to test assumptions and validate their decisions. Consultants receive a fee for their work.

A New Network

Prior to the 1980s, people visualized intermediaries as accountants with green visors in smoke filled back offices hammering out deals. The public could not differentiate among the various private equity professionals. Back then the infrastructure for buying businesses was limited. There were few private buyers and they were usually known to the seller. Owners worked at a successful business until they died and then it was left to their heirs to dispose of. Potential purchasers were usually local competitors. These limited borders have expanded and the net of private deals has been cast further afield.

Even in public equity at that time, there was a strong home bias: Canadians invested mainly in the Canadian stock market. This is no longer true; globalization has affected public and private markets. Investment advisors wouldn't think of recommending that clients buy mainly Canadian stocks. Canada has such a small percentage of world markets (around 4%) and its industry choices are limited (mainly oil & gas, mining, and banks). Even RRSP rules restricting the ownership of foreign stocks in retirement plans have been eliminated. The investment scope has broadened to take advantage of opportunities everywhere.

Similarly, some Canadian PE firms consider themselves North American or even global. In keeping with this broader mandate, the primary challenge for every PE firm buying businesses is 'deal flow' or finding the right businesses. When it comes to 'deal flow' on this enlarged playing field, M&A and consulting firms improve the efficiency of locating suitable businesses and aid in their seamless transfer. Private equity has spawned a whole network. Thus, business owners have more options and an improved distribution system when the time comes to sell.

22

Profitable Points

(The Go-Betweens: M&A Firms)

- *While PE firms act as principals, other professional groups such as M&A and consulting firms advise businesses and assist in the sale of a business.*

- *M&A firms are intermediaries who act as advisors for the business owner and prepare a company for financing, refinancing or a sale. Mainly M&A firms are paid a commission for meeting the vendor's objective.*

- *There are four events that trigger the involvement of an M&A firm: An owner wants to grow a business, sell a business, take out money or do succession planning.*

- *In addition, there are consultants who are hired to help a business solve problems and plan for growth. They are paid a fee for their time and effort.*

- *Consulting firms can be generalists and work with various objectives or can specialize in a defined area, such as due diligence.*

- *Because investing has become global, private business owners have an enlarged market for selling their businesses. Intermediaries improve the efficiency of private markets.*

RAISING FUNDS

*"Mutual fund performance is more about who's hot,
whereas private equity fund performance is more
about who's good."*

Mark Satov,
Satov Consulting Inc.

The first and least popular job in any PE firm is fundraising. Fundraising means what its name suggests: finding outside investors to commit money in order to create a pool of capital. If the PE firm succeeds it will establish a private equity fund (PE fund) and the money will be used to buy into a handful of private businesses. Fundraising is arduous and time consuming. A PE firm's main role, buying and building businesses is much more satisfying. Fundraising takes time away from the day-to-day activity of working with businesses and directing their growth. Ironically, it puts a PE firm on the opposite side of the fence: instead of providing money to businesses they must first ask investors for it.

Fundraising can take anywhere from three months to 18 months, depending on variables like market conditions and the economic situation. Investors pay some of their commitment into the fund immediately on signing the legal agreement; the rest is called for by the PE firm as needed. When the PE firm finds suitable investments, it draws down the balance of the committed money. It takes about three to five years before all the money committed to a PE fund is invested. Some call this period 'the investment period'.

Although the typical investment period is about five years, fundraising for the next fund starts after the PE firm has reached a threshold: say when 75% of capital is invested, then the process of raising money starts all over again. If the firm can make a good case for itself and has satisfied its outside investors, it solicits the same supporters for the next pool of capital and the start of a new fund. Typically, the next fund is started before the capital for the last fund is deployed.

In Canada, there are few PE firms that are more than four to five years old; so most of them are only on their first or second fund. To raise money for a fund, PE firms need a track record. In the U.S. the track record of professionals at PE firms is gained through experience at previous PE firms. Often these professionals break away and start their own firm. They rely on a track record built while working for someone else. In Canada, private equity is so new that often the track record of PE professionals comes from managing private businesses for wealthy families or for a Canadian bank.

As part of the fundraising, a PE firm drafts an 'offering' document which includes a business plan. Since it is asking for money to purchase businesses in the future, it develops a proposal for the types of businesses it plans to buy. For example, I spoke with a Canadian PE firm that concentrates on small businesses in southern Ontario. This particular PE firm limits itself to five businesses in a PE fund and excludes itself from investing in certain cyclical industries, such as real estate or mining.

The other part of the fundraising process is negotiating the partnership agreement between the PE firm and its investors. A partnership agreement defines the relationship between the general and limited partners. Partnership agreements, where LPs are not involved in business decisions, frees inactive investors from any liability claims other than their committed capital. The structure gives LPs the same protection that they would have as a public shareholder and ensures they are protected against any liability based on mismanagement within a company.

The partnership agreement also lays out the GP's fees, usually 2% of committed capital on an annual basis, plus a 20% 'carried interest' in the net profits of the investment pool when the businesses are sold. Therefore, the GP has both a regular income and a 'carried interest' which could put his needs at odds with the LPs. To avoid conflicts, restrictions are placed on GP behaviour. For example, to protect against undue risk-taking, when a business is sold, the agreement usually states that the LPs' original capital must be returned first.

In addition when businesses are sold, LPs are entitled to a reasonable rate of return that compensates them for the use of their capital. This occurs before the GP receives a 'carried interest' and is called the hurdle rate. The hurdle rate is a safeguard to ensure that the profit is large enough to compensate the LPs for their added risk. Once the GP exceeds the hurdle, the overall split of the profits becomes the 20% 'carried interest' for the PE firm and 80% for the investors. At its best, the annual fee covers the GPs' operating costs while the 'carried interest' motivates them to maximize the long-term profitability of the partnership.

Once the PE firm has invested all the money in a fund, it still needs several additional years to build and sell the businesses. PE funds have a finite lifetime, generally lasting 7-10 years with options for extensions. This means that PE firms try to sell all the businesses in a PE fund before the wind up date. Frequently, PE firms sell the businesses and return the fund's capital in half that time when possible. The partnership agreement sets a deadline to wind up, to sell the businesses and for all distributions.

The existence of a deadline or expiry date marks one of the major differences between private equity funds and stock market shareholders. In public markets, investors can hold stock for as long as they choose. It is not uncommon to own common stocks for 20 years or even pass them down to future generations. When I was an investment advisor, I often met people who inherited shares in listed companies: some of these shares had passed down through two or three generations with good returns. I met families with shares in Canadian banks or utilities where the shares had been in the family for generations and were a source of family pride and heritage. PE funds and the companies they invest in have a brief and fixed time to make their mark and move on.

This impermanent nature of private equity capital creates both business opportunities and disadvantages. An advantage is that there is a goal and a deadline. Therefore, businesses stay focused. The PE firms that control the businesses must execute their game plans to make a profit and raise money for their next funds. Private equity businesses claim that this helps them avoid many of the problems experienced by public shareholders who complain of waste, inefficiency and unproductive assets.

However, there may be a disadvantage to the business because businesses in a PE fund will be sold or refinanced within a relatively short period. This changes business thinking and the way it operates. How do you plan for long-term research or new ideas that do not fit the timeframe? How do you take a chance on an acquisition or experiment with new trends when the expiry date is looming? Do PE firms limit the vision of a business and encourage relatively short-term thinking? This last question is one of the most important and difficult issues in relation to the PE model. I return to it in the last section when I discuss the meltdown.

From the investor's point of view, private equity has other advantages. PE firms are pro-active and sometimes better representatives of their investors' goals than the executives and boards in listed companies. Based on their incentives, PE firms are focused on growing profits for the expiry date whereas executives and boards at listed companies have more varied objectives and responsibilities and so can easily lose focus and consistency.

There is also a disadvantage to investors. LPs cannot stay with businesses they like because these businesses must be sold within a short time frame. It is not uncommon for businesses in a fund to be sold within three years of purchase, less than one business cycle. As businesses are sold and PE funds wound up, LPs find themselves with a constant reinvestment problem. As their cash is returned, they must search for and investigate new opportunities. This is a time-consuming proposition involving due diligence and legal fees. It explains why fundraising is so frequent; PE firms come back to their investors with new funds to reinvest cash raised from businesses recently sold.

Finding solid businesses is not always easy. PE firms or their investors can hold uninvested money for long stretches. This narrows the thinking of PE firms to opportunities which have a chance of aggressive growth. They buy businesses if they estimate that, at the least, they will double or triple their investment; otherwise it is not worth tying up cash. This minimum requirement compensates for stretches when cash remains parked in short-term deposits. In other words, to allow for the disadvantage of poor short-term returns, PE firms pick businesses that can grow to two or three times their invested capital within a PE fund.

Currently, the majority of funds have a sizeable minimum dollar investment requirement which makes them unaffordable for most Canadian investors. Also, having money tied up for 7-10 years is too long for the average investor. Therefore, only institutions and wealthy individuals who can handle these barriers invest thorough PE funds. Currently, the majority of investors in PE funds are institutions such as pension funds. Some wealthy Canadian and foreign families are also participants.

These investors are discerning and have sufficient clout to negotiate advantageous partnership agreements. This is one reason that fundraising does not rate highly as a favourite activity. PE firms are forced to actively negotiate to win lead investors. Also, a partnership agreement must take into account the needs of different types of investors: such as foreign versus Canadian, taxable accounts versus non taxable accounts, different appetites for risk, and different economic cycles. These are not boilerplate agreements.

In the U.S. there are thousands of PE firms, whereas in Canada there are only a few hundred. This makes private equity much more competitive south of the border. In the U.S. there are placement agencies. These are companies who know all the institutions and wealthy investors and will bring together GPs and LPs. The placement agencies also vet the GPs for their authenticity. This provides a wider distribution and matchmaking service. In Canada, the industry is still so small that the PE firm professionals and LPs all seem to know each other.

27

There are ways to invest in private equity without committing daunting sums of money and being locked in for 7-10 years. Smaller investors can participate in private equity through publicly traded shares and mutual fund trusts. We will return to these different methods for taking advantage of private equity.

Profitable Points

(Raising Funds)

- *During fundraising, PE firms raise a pool of capital to purchase a handful of businesses. This capital constitutes a PE fund.*

- *It takes about 3-5 years for the PE firm to find suitable businesses to purchase. This is known as the 'Investment Period'.*

- *PE firms need to present a clear proposal outlining how the money will be spent and the types of businesses they are targeting. This is part of the 'offering' document that is prepared in order to raise money.*

- *The agreement that defines the relationship between the PE firm and its outside investors is called the partnership agreement. Most PE funds are structured as limited partnerships.*

- *Partnerships are composed of active partners (GPs) who manage the capital and advise the businesses plus inactive partners (LPs) who provide the capital.*

- *LPs who are not involved in business decisions have no liability for claims made against the individual businesses (i.e. limited liability).*

- *GPs receive 2% of committed capital as an annual fee and a 20% 'carried interest' in the overall profits of the partnership. The 2% covers their costs and the 20% is their incentive to grow the businesses.*

- *After the investment period, the PE firm takes several more years to build and sell the businesses. PE funds have a finite lifetime, usually 7-10 years, in which the fund must be wound up and the capital returned to the investors.*

CHASING DEALS: FINDING, MINDING AND GRINDING

"The three components of success for a private equity firm are sourcing a suitable deal, creating the right vision and being able to execute on that vision."

Brent S. Belzberg, Senior Managing Partner,
Torquest Partners

According to insiders, two trends in private equity are inevitable. PE firms will continue to expand in Canada because of growing demand. Secondly, there will be a shortage of professionals at the senior level. The skills required at the top take years to develop; they require deal-making capabilities, financial backgrounds and business operating experience. In Canada, it seems there will be a shortage of leadership with the necessary qualifications. Many ideal candidates, skillful at managing businesses, have no interest in PE firms. Overseeing several businesses at a time is hard work and being dependent on the 'carry' could mean an unreliable income.

From the investor's standpoint, tying up capital for 10 years in a fund seems like a long time. However, for a PE firm there are numerous obligations to fulfill during that time span. They must select businesses, negotiate the purchase, increase the value and arrange a profitable sale. The role of a PE firm partner is not conducive to a regular lifestyle. While I was writing this book and interviewing these professionals, I had a glimpse of the incessant travel, the juggling of schedules and the relentless time pressures demanded by their portfolio companies.

In order to relate to the challenges of partners in PE firms, it is necessary to understand the roles they perform during different periods or stages in a PE fund. There are three periods in a PE fund and PE firms must skillfully maneuver through all three: the investment period, the development period, and the harvest period. Although these three periods are sequential, they can overlap. This is because businesses are bought and sold at different times.

The Investment Period

After the investors' money is committed to a fund, a PE firm starts negotiating for appropriate businesses. Partners who hunt down viable deals are termed 'the finders'. Sourcing the right deals is a talent and many 'finders' specialize in this one task. The process is slow and it can take as long as three to five years to invest in a suitable basket of businesses. This includes spotting the deals, building the relationships and the arduous task of negotiating with business management. Sometimes the offer falls through or there is no agreement on price or management goes with another investor. A lot of work may be done with nothing to show for it. It is a trying procedure and requires a patient, stoical dedication.

The process of searching for businesses is an ongoing procedure. Even though PE firms do not negotiate for businesses until they have completed their fundraising, they are constantly on the lookout for businesses. Often partners build relationships with business owners and their advisors over decades before a potential deal is struck. Private equity is a relationship business where networking and bonding is crucial. A few partners in every firm are usually superior at building bridges to future deals.

'Deal flow' is the term that describes the long-term courting of businesses by PE firms. It is important not only because it aids in the purchase of businesses, but because it allows PE firms to learn about different industries, kick the tires and create a pipeline of opportunities.

There are two ways to generate 'deal flow': PE firms can locate businesses on their own or find businesses through auctions. One source for locating businesses on their own is the relationship with previous owners who have done business with a PE firm and bring new contacts. Sometimes business owners engage in more than one business and are themselves a source of several deals.

Once a PE firm becomes a business owner within an industry, similar businesses tend to be offered to the firm. As the PE firm builds its network with various executives, managers and other insiders, these individuals spot new opportunities and are a source of deals. In addition, competitors in the industry may contact the PE firm to inquire about selling their business.

PE firms are enthusiastic about deals brought to them by business managers who would like to buy out existing owners. They are delighted to finance and partner with an established management team. When times are slow, PE firms are proactive, telephoning owners and managers about buying their business.

Deals that a PE firm finds on its own are called proprietary deals. This is a continuous, long-term, business building strategy central to the existence of a PE firm. Next to fundraising, developing the right connections to maintain the 'deal flow' is probably the most important task of a PE firm. It is the choice way to find deals because PE firms have an inside track and have more time to understand the business.

The second source of business deals is through auctions arranged by other financial professionals, such as advisors at accounting firms or M&A firms. These are silent auctions where the business accepts offers from a variety of bidders including PE firms, other investors and competitors.

Usually PE firms try to avoid auctions because they must work through third parties. Therefore they lack the close connections and deep insights gained by finding their own proprietary deals. Also, a business sold through auction is completed over a short time period so PE firms don't have as much time to study the business. Much as PE firms would like to depend on their own proprietary deals, the more competitive the market, the more businesses are sold through silent auctions.

The Development Period

Because PE firms have only a relatively short time to enhance the value of a business, they must have a fundamental understanding of how businesses work. Each time a PE firm buys a business, it has to absorb a new operating philosophy, environment, business culture, assortment of systems and procedures. Also, personal chemistry problems are almost certain to arise as outsiders try to integrate with existing management and personnel. A criticism often leveled at PE firms is that they are composed of too many financial people incapable of adapting to intricate business environments. For this reason, many PE firms include professionals with operating experience.

Sometimes the job of building businesses is accomplished because PE firms specialize in specific industries/services where they develop sufficient expertise to evaluate a company's unique value. Rarely do their original plans materialize as smoothly as anticipated; hence PE firms stalk businesses which have a niche and a one or two year lead time on their competition. The private equity professionals supply the vision which is coupled with the business management's own financial and technical skill to execute on the game plan. Well laid out financials and reasonable growth projections keep the business recruits on track and allow professionals at the PE firm to keep score.

It takes a special prowess to deal with the unknowns of a new business, grow it to a higher level and prepare it for a profitable sale. PE firms must be good at accessing outside professionals and business experts to help build their portfolio companies. Often such outsourced professionals are 'serial entrepreneurs' who have succeeded in previous businesses and are in search of new outlets for their energy and expertise. They bring strategic contacts and a network they employ in each new business. These experts know when the numbers or financials of a target company make sense. Most do their own projections and evaluations.

Despite diligent selection, people, plans and ideas are hard to evaluate and even professionals can misjudge the expertise of a founder or management team. In addition, the market may not be as easy to penetrate as they expected and the technology not as good as they thought. In the insightful words of Benjamin Graham, "Obvious prospects for physical growth in a business do not translate into obvious profits for investors."[5] Failure to execute on one component of a business system in a growing competitive environment dramatically alters the chances of success. This is why there are a number of business failures among private equity portfolios. Many outstanding PE firms have earned their reputations by developing the internal depth and breadth to optimize businesses through the challenging development stage.

In Canada, expertise in specific industries is particularly difficult to develop because of the small market. Not only is our market small, but it lacks the diversity of businesses found in the U.S. This means that there are several good businesses where no Canadian PE firms are available with enough experience to finance and grow the business. Often, these businesses turn to the United States for advice, funding, and support.

If you examine large Canadian private equity deals, such as Shoppers Drug Mart or Yellow Pages, the businesses' internal structure is highly developed. There are several layers of management and a good hierarchy for making decisions. These businesses have systems and procedures that are sophisticated and up to date. The PE firms that purchased them could afford to hire top outside consultants to find and solve problems without disrupting the existing business. These businesses have enterprise values in excess of $2 billion, very rare by Canadian standards.

In contrast, most Canadian businesses are valued at less than $50 million. Such businesses lack the depth of management and a chain of command for decision making. Often the technology, systems and procedures are inadequate. They tend to require hands-on help and day to day involvement from buyers. Smaller and mid-size businesses need Canadian PE firms with a local knowledge situated within the businesses' vicinity for regular contact. A few

---

5. Benjamin Graham, *The Intelligent Investor* (New York: Harper & Row, 1973).

Canadian PE firms insist that the businesses they purchase must be located within a three-hour drive to ensure frequent meetings.

GPs and LPs both contribute capital to a PE fund with the goal of creating common vested interests and sharing risks and rewards. In the same way, executives in their newly acquired business are expected to buy equity. Executives must also share the risks and rewards. This is an 'alignment of interests' between GPs, investors and executives so that their interests are intertwined and they are motivated towards the same ends.

Since the 'alignment of interests' stretches from private equity partners through to key management, there tends to be a disciplined hierarchy. This arrangement, where everyone invests their hard-earned cash, inspires trust and better harmony. Key people don't second-guess each others' motives. PE firms can maintain tight control over the boards and implement strong governance systems. They often have a better handle on spending, a superior strategic plan and more accountability from management than do listed companies.

Because PE firms invest through funds that only remain as owners for a short stint, it is necessary to keep employees motivated and running hard. The development period is based on a simple premise; by insisting that everyone capable of making a difference to the bottom line purchase equity, a PE firm can motivate people and drive them hard for about five years until the business is profitably sold. Then they all reap their proportionate share of the net profits.

The Harvest Period

The last stage consists of harvesting (exiting) the individual businesses. There are a variety of ways to exit or sell the businesses in a fund. PE firms can locate a strategic buyer, which is a business owner in the same industry interested in merging. This allows a competitor to buy a portfolio company and expand. Alternatively, a PE firm can find a financial buyer, which is an individual or group interested in a portfolio company as an investment.

If a business has grown sufficiently, a PE firm can approach an investment dealer or brokerage house to launch an IPO (Initial Public Offering). In an IPO, the business is sold on the stock market. There is constant interchange between private and public equity. Large private businesses can be sold on stock markets. Meanwhile, public corporations or their divisions are bought by PE firms, given the right opportunity. The process resembles a pendulum.

If a business has grown and has adequate cash flow, the exiting management can try and obtain financing in order to take the business to the next level. It is not unusual for business management to find a new partner and buy the business for itself in a 'management buyout'.

The strategy that PE firms employ depends on market conditions at the time of the disposition. If the exit climate is favourable they might enjoy multiple buyers and a sizeable premium increase on their original purchase price. Also, when interest rates fall, sale prices and premiums tend to increase, because purchases are cheaper to finance. Unfortunately, the opposite also holds true.

One final way of repaying investors is called 'recapitalization'. If a business succeeds in paying down part of its debt or can support a larger debt burden, then the investment can be refinanced, thereby releasing some of the cash back to the original investors. If this happens early in the life of an investment, then it is a windfall because investors reduce the money they have tied up in a deal.

In contrast, when a sale is inopportune, 'recapitalization' of a business gives investors money back while they await a favourable exit opportunity. The better the earnings growth the more flexible the available options to reward investors anticipating a final sale.

In summary, although money invested in a PE fund for 10 years seems like a long time, the PE firm has a demanding agenda. It must identify and attract new opportunities, negotiate purchases, monitor and oversee existing businesses, and orchestrate opportune exit strategies to dispose of businesses.

Profitable Points

(Chasing Deals: Finding, Minding and Grinding)

- *There are three stages in a PE fund: the investment period, the development period and the harvest period. Although these three periods are sequential they can overlap because several businesses are being bought and sold at different times.*

- *The investment period is the time when PE firms negotiate for and purchase a handful of businesses for a PE fund.*

- *'Deal flow' is the term that describes the long-term courting of businesses by PE firms. It is a continuous, business building strategy central to the existence of a PE firm.*

- *There are two sources of deals: Deals that PE firms find on their own are called proprietary deals. Alternatively, deals that are brought to them by intermediaries such as accounting firms and M&A firms require PE firms to bid in an auction.*

- *The development period is when PE firms build and grow businesses. In order to add value to a business within its relatively short time frame, PE firms must hit the ground running. Therefore, private equity has spawned 'serial entrepreneurs', professionals who have succeeded in previous businesses and can deal with the unknowns of a new business. They bring strategic knowhow and networks to each new undertaking.*

- *A noteworthy advantage of private equity, particularly during the development period, is the alignment of interests between GPs, LPs and business executives. This is because all three parties are expected to invest in order to share similar risks and rewards. Hence, PE firms have a better handle on a strategic plan and exert greater influence towards growth than their stock market competition.*

- *The last period is the harvest period when businesses are sold or wound up.*

- *PE firms exit their investments by selling the individual businesses. There are two types of buyers: strategic investors operating in the same industry or financial buyers searching for profitable investments. In addition, businesses can be launched as IPOs and sold on public stock markets.*

- *If market conditions do not favour a sale, a growing business can be refinanced, so that money is taken out of the business and returned to the investors.*

- *It takes approximately ten years from the beginning to the close of a PE fund. During this time the PE firm selects businesses, negotiates purchases, oversees its businesses in order to grow them and finds the right point to sell each business.*

THE FIRST 100 DAYS

*"Many a private equity firm could avoid failure in a
portfolio company by moving in the first 100 days to
accelerate their strategic plan."*

Ryan Brain, Partner, Financial Advisory,
Deloitte & Touche LLP

Do PE firms really add value to the businesses they buy? This is a hot
topic and has been the subject of articles and books. Perhaps the verdict is not in
yet because private equity is so untested, particularly in Canada. Some even
argue that the post-2007 meltdown will prove that private equity offers a superior business model.

PE firms can bring outside perspective that the old executive team does
not have. They can tease out fundamental strategic questions and add value that
a busy management team in the daily trenches hasn't time for. Before a decision
can be made regarding the value added, it is necessary to understand the PE
firm's approach to a new acquisition.

There are two ways a business can grow after a purchase by a PE firm.
The first is the organic way, meaning without help or interference. PE firms
cherry pick and buy businesses that already have a lead on the competition.
Usually, these businesses have momentum and grow independently for a
period of time.

In a good economy, this strategy works well. Under its existing structure,
a business is likely to evolve and grow spontaneously. However, in difficult
times, this strategy can be disastrous. Thriving businesses deteriorate rapidly
and can fail without the PE firm's intervention. In a challenging, hostile environment, PE firms can't depend on coasting and financial engineering. The
debt applied to business cash flow to fund the purchase can start to work against
the survival of the business.

The second way of growing involves an action plan with good execution.
PE firms have an investment thesis before they buy a business. Prior to a purchase, a PE firm performing its due diligence becomes familiar with both the
risks and rewards of the business under consideration. It enters into a deal
aware of the shortcomings and with a reasonable expectation of the issues that
lie ahead. During due diligence it can build a proactive investment thesis. Prior
to closing, it would have a blueprint for growth. The investment thesis can target internal growth whereby a business finds ways to improve its existing sales

and operations. Alternatively, an investment thesis can be directed toward external expansion through outside acquisitions.

The reason for the sale to a PE firm determines the challenges it will face. Businesses are sold for two main reasons; in the first, the previous owners are leaving. For example, in succession planning, previous owners have taken the business as far as they can go and the PE firm must replace the owners and grow the business to the next level.

In the second case, the owners want to stay and partner with a PE firm in order to grow. Here, the existing management has presented an idea that makes sense and a PE firm has decided to run with it. The PE firm buys into the business to inject new resources. In either situation, the action plan comes out of this discovery process and the first 100 days should offer new perspectives and new tools to take the business to the next level.

Never has a proactive plan been more important than in the post 2007 environment. Ironically, consultants interviewed suggest this is not the Canadian way. One international consulting firm indicated that in the U.K., PE firms consistently have a detailed post acquisition plan built on best practices, whereas only a handful of Canadian PE firms could claim the same. In general, Canadian PE firms have kept hands off, not wanting to stir the pot.

When I questioned the logic, I was offered a couple of reasons. Canadian PE firms do not like to be disruptive. The growth in Canadian private equity is so recent that investment returns were good without active intervention. However, this passive method will present a greater challenge down the road.

The second reason for the 'hands off' policy pertains to reputational risk. Canadian PE firms are afraid to be labeled as difficult with the repercussions this could have on future purchases. Potential vendors might not sell to PE firms which they perceive as disruptive.

Those consultants experienced with the failure of portfolio businesses question this passive approach. In each and every failed case, they say the PE firm wishes it had moved more quickly towards their investment plan. It was clear from their due diligence what needed to happen but the PE firm either acted too slowly or ignored the issue once the deal closed. Investment plans can contain unpalatable decisions which the PE firm could not face, such as job cuts or factory closings. It seems PE firms are subject to human failings; strategic plans are not translated into actions, and by the time change comes it is too late.

During the first 100 days, a PE firm needs to decide: "How do you extract more value from the business and make it a better business?" In the past, some Canadian PE firms counted on financial engineering, such as re-jigging the balance sheet or adding debt. After the downturn, the consensus is that PE firms will have to reorient and grow businesses, not just tweak them at the edges, to produce a profit within their limited time span.

Prior to announcing a purchase, PE firms tread lightly. Not everyone in the acquired business knows that a transition is coming. The PE firm does not want to be intrusive. Employees have set ways of doing things and change can be disruptive. Once the purchase is official, change can't be prolonged and must be dealt with quickly, preferably within 100 days. Ultimately, this impacts morale favourably because employees often rally once their own situation is clear.

Although PE firms are not looking to strip responsibilities from management, after a purchase, priorities often change. Employees usually expect change with new ownership. To reduce uncertainty, a PE firm must identify the problems, transmit their new vision and signal their direction. Management and employees are usually primed for an overhaul and the first 100 days are the best opportunity to outline any new objectives.

In speaking with consultants, I found they were helpful in explaining the methodology of a 100-day plan. When a PE firm buys a business, the first step is to acknowledge the issues and risks. What did they learn when they were deciding to make their purchase? Then they develop a dialogue with those in charge. Out of this, an agenda evolves that establishes priorities and determines what should be done, when and by whom.

Taking possession of new businesses is not simple and there are common post-acquisition problems. A PE firm is juggling short-term issues while grappling with longer term strategic directions. The PE firm wants to secure its new asset while moving forward. Consider these five areas where a PE firm could fall short.

People—Usually, PE firms do not get involved with individual employees. Key people may not be identified until too late. Defections are a common by-product of new ownership. I heard about a top sales person who left soon after a deal closed, taking all his customer relationships with him.

Financial reporting—PE firms are excellent at doing the financial analysis to buy a business, but this is a one-time effort. Meanwhile, they can be slow to change the reporting standards to make way for new ownership.

This makes it difficult to track business during transition and afterwards. When PE firms are not close to daily operations, they may not identify issues and challenges soon enough. A common cause of post-acquisition failure is inadequate reporting.

Operational issues—Operational issues are an on-going, day-to-day challenge. They are particularly difficult when a new ownership is trying to implement change. I heard of a business that decided to consolidate operations in a central location; however, excessive time was taken to close costly outlying warehouses.

Customer base—It is hard for a PE firm to understand the strength or security of the customer base. Often PE firms don't communicate directly with customers. Therefore, they do not know where they are exposed and what the competition is doing to lure them away.

Controls—There needs to be a whole new system of written procedures to reflect new governance. Implementation and oversight can be very difficult for a PE firm that doesn't know the ropes. For example, who accepts credit risks and signs cheques? Is this acceptable to the new owners?

In the longer term, a PE firm must understand the competitive advantage of a business in order to grow. Why has the business been successful in the past and what is its sustainable competitive advantage? A business has only one or two things that give it an edge: best-known brand, the biggest chain, cutting-edge technology, best sales team, or quality reputation. A business can have several fine qualities, but many are just icing.

PE firms that can't clearly pinpoint the competitive advantage of the businesses they buy can't expand on its strength. Some businesses will never outlive their original owners. At the same time, a business executive and management team that has grown up with the same vision has a limited perspective. The future can lie with the fresh thinking and resources of a PE firm. Experienced PE firms can bring in new ideas and additional capital to raise the CEO and management team up to the next rung, but it is not easy. This is where the best PE firms add value and produce outstanding returns.

Profitable Points

(The First 100 Days)

- *Good PE firms have the time and inclination to address strategic questions in a portfolio business. They can bring outside perspective and resources that the old business executive team did not have.*

39

- *After a business is purchased, it can continue to grow without help from the PE firm for a period of time. Some PE firms depend on this for their profit.*

- *Alternatively, a PE firm can develop an action plan with new perspectives and tools to take the business to the next level. This can be done within the first 100 days.*

- *Experts experienced with the reasons for failure of portfolio businesses, claim that the PE firm in charge usually moved too slowly or ignored their investment plan after taking over a business.*

- *When a PE firm purchases a business, employees expect change. So change must be dealt with quickly to keep morale high.*

- *Taking possession of a business is not easy and there are common post-acquisition problems. These problems revolve around employees, financial reporting, operational issues, the customer base, and controls.*

- *A business has only one or two things that give it an edge. For example, the best known brand, the biggest size, cutting edge technology, best sales team, or a quality reputation. The best PE firms pinpoint the competitive advantage in order to expand and grow the business.*

SECTION II: THE CRAFT

THE STRUGGLE FOR CAPITAL: VENTURE VERSUS BUYOUT

"Public equity is about safeguarding the assets;
Private equity is about increasing the value."

Don McLauchlin, Vice President,
Roynat Capital

The Contenders

There are two main categories of private equity: venture and buyout. PE firms specialize in one or the other. The problem is that even the experts disagree on an exact definition for the two terms. This is because both venture and buyout are made up of several stages and it is hard to determine where various stages begin, end or overlap.

Moreover, the skills needed to select and oversee venture businesses vs. buyouts are very different. Therefore, each PE firm has it own internal definition. For our purposes, venture businesses are high growth, young businesses that are not yet established and commonly not revenue-producing. In contrast, buyouts are later-stage, mature businesses that are revenue-producing and typically are profitable. In the life cycle of a business, there is also a start-up stage (prior to venture) where PE firms fear to tread.

If you understand the growth stages of a business then you will begin to understand the challenges that different PE firms face as they invest in businesses and attempt to add value.

Angel Investing

The earliest investors in a company are called 'angels'. Angels provide money for start-up companies. This is the 'extreme sport' of investing because the businesses have no track record. Rarely will professional investors get involved this early, so the main investors other than the owners themselves are family and friends enticed by their enthusiasm. These investors have been dubbed the "Three F's" (family, fools, and friends). Usually the amounts of money invested are small and the businesses are also tiny, with less than 20 employees. Angels hope to profit in start-ups by taking an ownership position. Debt financing is not an option since start-ups do not have stable cash flow to make interest payments.

41

Venture Capital

Venture capital begins when companies grow to a stage where PE firms are prepared to make a commitment. There are many stages to venture, and various PE firms are intent on different entry points. Some professionals get involved early, once there is a glimmer of hope and call their initial foray, "seed capital", a subset of venture. Many early-stage businesses do not yet produce a product or provide a service and therefore attract little interest. However, once a product is developed and/or a business has a source of revenue, PE firms specializing in venture will step up to the plate and interest spreads.

Because so many venture businesses are new, small and rarely profitable, evaluating them is more art than science and they are selected based on instinct and experience. Venture capitalists know how to run a business and many are entrepreneurs who have succeeded at previous endeavors. If their investee businesses hit a road block, venture investors have management capabilities available to step in and clear the impasse. The best private equity venture firms help build a business. They are partners, not just moneymen.

How do venture capitalists choose from the vast array of hopefuls seeking funding? They target businesses that can grow quickly and grow to a significant size. Such businesses serve large or mass markets and are inherently less risky than catering to a small niche. Venture professionals employ keen market instincts to determine if the product or service is commercially viable for a large scale market.

Despite the impression that venture capital is provided to the best ideas or most charismatic entrepreneurs, in reality investment flows to high-growth market sectors with good near term prospects. A good sector is forgiving and allows room for inefficiency. Management can be replaced or fixed while it is carried along by a moving tide. As for ideas, they want commercial applications of existing technologies. As one venture professional joked, "They can't wait for a solution in search of a problem". Timing is critical. PE firms try to enter a market ripe for take-off and exit just as the market matures and profit margins are squeezed.

A descriptive word used in venture circles is the word 'incubate' which conveys what good venture capitalists do. They embed themselves in the company, nurture and fill in the missing management. They are engrossed in soft issues like the quality of key management and the demand for the product or service. The hardcore issues involve due diligence of the intellectual property and background checks of key employees.

A distinct feature of venture specialists is that they do not normally take a majority position in the companies in which they invest. Since the risk of failure in venture companies is so high, they want key people who are personally on the line if the enterprise fails. This is colourfully described as "having skin in the game".

The odds are stacked against venture capital investors, so they demand a high potential return on their capital. This creates a delicate balancing act between the right incentives for the business entrepreneurs and proper rewards for venture capitalists. Venture capital is high growth, but high risk. In Canada, there has been much recent press suggesting that capital allocated to venture has been shrinking and is increasingly difficult to find. In mature markets, like the U.S. and U.K., 75%-80% of PE firms focus on the next stage, buyouts.

Buyout

In contrast to venture, buyout PE firms set their sights on established businesses. Candidates are larger, more mature and require less hand-holding. Buyout businesses are more valuable and command a premium. The skills required in buyout transactions are unique to this particular stage. This tends to be a numbers game with less art and more science. Entrants come from an accounting or investment background where mathematical aptitudes are essential. Buyouts require serious financial analysis.

In addition, buyout specialists operate in more traditional businesses. They lack the nose of venture professionals for new market trends. Their businesses have arrived and the numbers confirm whether a potential acquisition is growing. It is not as necessary to rely on instinct.

Buyout candidates have a predictable history of sales and earnings and sufficient cash flow to service interest payments and to repay principal. This is a distinguishing feature of a buyout transaction since the newly purchased business may be saddled with increased debt used to finance their acquisition by the PE firm.

Why submit to a buyout? Often the business is expanding, acquiring another business, or itself being taken over by new management as in the case of retiring owners. Sometimes divisions of large corporations are spun off, allowing the parent to focus on its core business. These are all opportunities where the business eventually expects to increase revenue, earnings or both.

Buyout specialists tear apart the numbers and restructure bank debt to maximize any financing possibilities. Banks are leery of high levels of operating debt, so the first step in any buyout is consolidating existing debt and redeploying the debt in order to maximize future borrowing potential. This is where the creativity occurs. Whereas venture businesses are usually needy and do not qualify for debt, buyout financing depends on the skillful use of debt (or leverage).

A major difference between buyout firms and venture firms revolves around majority control. A buyout signals a change of ownership. Whereas venture firms want to partner with the existing business owners, buyout firms seek control. The PE firm is paying a premium to buy an established business and the assets will serve as security for their debt.

Since a buyout involves a takeover and replacing the previous owners, it is customary for key executives/management to be retained for the continuity of the business. PE firms work to secure these existing key people prior to any purchase. Management is normally comprised of several people who must be retained for the ultimate success of the takeover. These individuals sign agreements which hold the team in place for a period of time. In return, they are rewarded with options or earned equity when targets are met. This aligns the goals of business management with the PE firm.

The ultimate prize in a buyout is the cash flow. Hence, the primary goal when negotiating a purchase is to ensure that the cash flow estimates are accurate. If a buyout firm correctly predicts the cash flow and controls its use then it cannot be as easily misdirected in a manner which will jeopardize interest and principal payments. This reduces potential loss. The intelligent management of cash flow is also the source of future profits.

PE firms have come under fire for their use of debt in buyouts. There is the misconception that a buyout specialist merely loads a choice business with debt, sits back and waits for the earnings to grow. This belittles the complex skills involved in a successful deal. First there is the analysis of cash flow and restructuring of debt. Once this is accomplished the landscape keeps changing. The fortunes of the business change with its industry and the economy. The debt must be monitored and managed as interest rates change. In this fluctuating environment, even the best-laid numbers become unreliable. At the same time, a buyout firm grapples with cost-cutting and streamlining operations.

In the uncertainty created by a change of ownership, the big challenge is to make the earnings grow. Sometimes, there can be a trade-off between investing for longer term growth which can be costly or turning a quick profit. A company loaded with debt is a risky proposition, but to succeed in the long-term a company depends on superior growth of earnings, which requires investment. Deciding how to deploy cash, when to grow and where to cut requires astute and agile decision-making. This is where a superior PE firm excels; in allocating capital efficiently and providing oversight. Unlike venture, buyout candidates have different layers of management along with internal systems for managing their businesses. Therefore, PE firms offer less hands-on management and concentrate on effective financing and earnings growth.

It is sometimes difficult to draw a line in the sand and know when one stage ends and another begins. What venture and buyout have in common is a specific agenda: Both are focused on a window of opportunity and helping a company arrive at a new level. Venture specialists target young, high growth businesses. Buyout firms help mature businesses reach a new plateau. Neither venture nor buyout intends to remain with an investee business for its lifetime. Generally, buyouts aim for a three-year holding period and venture for five years.

Profitable Points

(The Struggle for Capital: Venture versus Buyout)

- *The earliest investors in a new business are called angels because they finance start-ups where the chances of success are slim. PE firms are rarely interested at this preliminary stage. Therefore, angel investing depends on personal acquaintances and relationships.*

- *PE firms divide private equity into two main categories: venture capital, which involves early stage growth companies that are not yet profitable and buyouts, which are larger established companies, capable of generating steady cash flow.*

- *The major financing instrument in venture capital is ownership. Venture companies can't afford interest payments on loans because they lack cash flow. In contrast, buyouts are almost always financed with debt.*

- *Venture investors partner with existing management in order to get the company off the ground and avoid failure. In contrast, a buyout signals a change of ownership. In a buyout the PE firm concentrates on making the best use of the financial resources of the business they have purchased and oversees the management and physical resources.*

THE GENIUS OF FINANCING

I have always been fascinated by money; mere slips of paper issued by a central authority, easily debased, devalued and counterfeited yet capable of directing our daily lives. It is an illusionary world. But, nowhere is its ingenuity more apparent than in the world of finance.

Despite temporary reversals, the growing sophistication of financial vehicles has resulted in an explosion of global commerce and wealth. New breakthroughs like microfinance have touched even the world's poorest denizens. This cousin of private equity merited a Nobel Peace Prize in 2006 for its founder Muhammad Yunus; a rare honor for a commercial concept. His initiative created financing opportunities for the world's poorest entrepreneurs, mainly women, in tiny cottage industries.

Private equity offers good examples of current financial efficiency. In any financial transaction, there are only two instruments for gain: debt instruments which offer interest payments, or ownership which offers profit potential. In private equity, the challenge lies in the skillful combinations geared to each situation. Since venture candidates cannot afford interest payments, their goal is to reward investors with equity while leaving sufficient ownership to motivate the original entrepreneurs. Buyout candidates can afford interest payments, but their goal is to avoid the rocky road to bankruptcy due to increased debt payments while still spending enough to grow the company.

Venture Capital

In a prior section, I referred to the main categories of private equity: venture and buyout. I described venture companies as young, high growth and not yet established. They lack the cash flow to fund their own development. These are the companies that require early stage financing. Companies at an early stage rarely have assets that can be sold if the business fails to meet its obligations; therefore the only potential source of gain is an ownership stake in the new business. This applies to all the subsets of venture, such as seed capital, angel investing and venture itself. At these stages, the company trades ownership for cash.

The faster a business is expanding, the more relentless its drive for money. With every growth spurt it taps investors for additional financing and each new infusion of cash is called 'a Round'. Like a developing embryo, after every financing round the company is bigger, more established and the ultimate chance of success is greater. The earliest investors take the biggest risk and face a reduced ownership percentage (called dilution) after each financing.

For example, assume Investor A contributes all the money to start a business and therefore owns 100%. When the developing business needs a second round of financing, Investor B steps in and contributes the same amount of money as his predecessor. Investor B now owns 50% of the company and Investor A's ownership is reduced from 100% to 50%. This is known as dilution and can be a major drawback for investors in venture capital.

Early investors who do not participate in future rounds will see their ownership stakes automatically dwindle. Even worse, if a business fails to perform and drops in value, future investors pay less for their stake. The original investor's stake is 'crushed'; not only does he own a smaller percentage, but it is worth less. For this reason, many venture capitalists abandon their worst performing start-ups and redeploy their capital elsewhere rather than participate in future rounds.

The main incentive for investing early is that an investor can take a meaningful position at a low price. If an investor is fortunate enough to select a business bound for success, participation becomes more expensive with each financing round. Where a business is ultimately successful, early investors enjoy the biggest percentage gain on their invested capital.

Different rounds of financing have different names (rounds A, B, C) and each round can have different rights, called class rights. Also, because the same investors do not necessarily participate in the various rounds, investors in different rounds can have different class rights.

For example, investors hoping to gain a bigger advantage can negotiate for shares that include warrants, rights, or convertible stock. These are perks similar to the coupons you receive at a local supermarket. They allow you to buy more shares at a special price in the future. They even have an expiry date. There is no lack of imagination when it comes to creating varying terms.

Hungry businesses tap every available source of capital, including suppliers who can participate by delaying inventory payments. For suppliers, this promotes their product while helping a new business preserve cash. No line of credit is ignored. However, despite all efforts, early-stage investing is very risky and therefore an expensive source of capital for a young business. Early investors or business founders often have to relinquish a high percentage of their shares (or equity) in order to obtain funding.

47

There are many tales of woe told by early investors who complain that they were forced to barter away the lion's share of their ownership in order to receive additional cash. Hence, when the business was finally sold, they had little to show for their original investment.

Still the odds are equally poor for PE firms that fund these ventures. It is estimated that 50% of all start-ups will fail to turn a profit. Statistically, at least 10% of businesses default, wiping out their entire capital, others just scrape along. A venture specialist described 95% of businesses in venture portfolios as 'walking wounded'; suggesting that overall most businesses neither make nor lose money for their investors.

The remaining 5% of businesses are such stars that they compensate for all the others. This is typical of venture portfolios and the professionals refer to their stars as 'Home Runs'. A 'Home Run' is defined as a portfolio company that returns the entire capital of its portfolio at least once.

To illustrate, assume a private equity venture firm raises $1 million for a PE fund and invests in 10 businesses. One of those businesses must be sold for $1 million in order to generate a reasonable rate of return, assuming that the other 9 businesses underperform or fail completely. Without one 'Home Run', venture is not worth the risk.

Based on its 'Home Runs', a few venture firms have succeeded in dramatically out- performing conventional investments. It is tantamount to creating a blockbuster in the movie theatre.

The goal of every venture firm is to own a stable of businesses in a portfolio that will produce at least one 'Home Run'. This Darwinian process must be ruthless to succeed. A professional must decide when to bail out of a struggling company in order to support another potential winner. With each financing round, professionals need capital to build their stake in their best choices and avoid dilution. Otherwise, they end up owning minor positions in a 'Home Run' and a basket of struggling start-ups. Obviously, this is a recipe for mediocre or negative performance.

I am in awe of the skill involved in picking a new business whose chances of success are slim, supporting and nurturing it until it is capable of competing efficiently; meanwhile, juggling a portfolio of striving enterprises with the goal of grooming those destined for success and eliminating those that fall behind.

Debt financing is only available when a company produces a stable cash flow and has the ability to service debt. There are also forms of financing, such as mezzanine financing, which offer a combination of both elements: debt and equity.

Mezzanine Financing

Unlike businesses in need of early stage financing, mid and later stage businesses have sufficient cash flow to pay regular interest and have some history of sales and revenue. There is not necessarily a progression from one stage to the next, and businesses like people can fall on hard times. However, once a business generates steady cash flow, the funding alternatives are vastly improved.

Structurally, mezzanine financing bridges a gap between financing with equity and financing with debt. Common shares, or ownership, offer no guarantee to investors of profit; senior debt financing (which is usually held by a bank) in addition to interest payments has a claim on collateral and is repaid first in case of default.

Mezzanine financing is junior debt, meaning holders are entitled to what is left over after senior debt holders have been repaid. In addition, mezzanine typically provides warrants. These are certificates that give investors a chance to buy shares in a business for a predetermined price over a given period. The combined interest payments from the mezzanine debt and estimated profit from the warrants are crafted to give the investor a tempting rate of return.

As a rough example, assume the going bank rate on financing (without collateral) is 12%, which is onerous for a growing business. 'Canadian Winner' (a mythical company) is on the verge of a significant breakthrough and needs money to expand. It approaches a PE firm that will provide mezzanine financing. The firm will lend money at 8% and receive warrants that permits it to buy a certain number of Canadian Winner common shares for up to two years at a 10% discount to their current price.

Mezzanine financing is a hybrid between debt and equity. For existing shareholders, it limits dilution of their current equity. The advantage to the business is that it pays a lower than normal interest rate on junior debt by including warrants that can be converted into equity. This reduces their costs and thereby provides breathing room. If this allows 'Canadian Winner' to become a larger more profitable business, it is win-win all around.

Buyout Financing

The last financing is a buyout. Whereas venture firms have several rounds of financing, buyout firms have only one because buyout firms take control of a business. The financing challenge in a buyout involves supplementing their available cash with funds borrowed against the collateral of the target company. The greater the proportion of debt the bigger the return the buyout firm earns by leveraging its capital.

For example, if a business is bought for $1 million and sold for $2 million and financed with the buyout firm's own cash its profit is 100%. However, if the buyout firm invests only $500,000 and borrows the rest against the candidate's assets and the business is sold for $2 million, the buyout firm earns 300%. The risks and rewards of leveraged buyouts are exponential. Like fireworks, the effects are explosive.

Experts argue over financing different business stages; whether it is worth investing in venture vs. buyouts. This is partly due to the bursting of the high tech bubble in March, 2000 when venture capital earned a bad reputation. Too many inadequate, overvalued businesses with unproven concepts, generating no revenue were packaged into PE funds.

Many of the businesses failed and the PE firms that supported them had dismal returns. In the U.S. the number of PE firms dedicated to venture capital has decreased significantly. This highlights the financing challenge of venture capital; valuations are dependent on instinct, timing and experience.

In contrast, buyouts in Canada between 2002 through 2006 produced an average annual return of 23.7% vs. 10.7% for an index that tracks the Toronto Stock Exchange (TSX).[6] This is the first time that such five-year numbers were compiled in Canada. Canadian institutional investors only became active in buyout around 2000, so some argue that they avoided the carnage of the dot.com bubble and were able to invest at the bottom of the market.

Unfortunately, because of a lack of reporting standards in Canadian private equity, these numbers are unaudited, but irresistible. Based on these numbers, Canada is off to a flying start.

Profitable Points
(The Genius of Financing)
- *The two tools of any financing are debt and equity; success in private equity transactions revolves around the skillful combination of these two instruments.*

---

6. *Private Equity Canada*, McKinsey & Company, Thomson Financial Canada.

- *In early financing, such as venture, businesses offer equity in exchange for capital. Early investors have the best opportunity for large percentage gains on invested capital, but often they face several financing rounds with the threat of dilution.*

- *Venture financing is high risk and only 5% of investments are likely to achieve success. These are called 'Home Runs'.*

- *When businesses have reached beyond venture where they can afford interest payments, then they qualify for mezzanine financing. In order to reduce their interest rates they include some form of equity (usually warrants).*

- *Because a buyout signals a change of ownership, there is only one financing round. Buyouts are financed with debt and the business is used as collateral for the loan. This is known as a leveraged buyout.*

- *Venture businesses are valued based on instinct, timing and experience. Buyouts are valued based on the cash flow generated by a business. Therefore, it is easier to establish objective standards for investing in buyouts.*

CASH FLOW: THE LIFEBLOOD OF PRIVATE EQUITY

The most venerated term in private equity is cash flow. It is the lifeblood of a private equity investment because it not only sustains the businesses but is also the source of rewards to the investors. While public investors can sell their investment whenever they wish on the stock market, private investors have no easy way of cutting their losses or reaping their reward. Instead, private investors are dependent on cash flows from the businesses owned by the PE fund and on the willingness of the PE firm to distribute some of the cash flows to investors. The problem is that neither the timing nor amount of payment is predictable. It is this uncertainty that makes private equity an unpalatable proposition for many investors.

Uncertainty also means that the returns on private equity investments are difficult to measure until a business is sold and the money distributed. Unlike listed companies, annual private equity returns are unreliable guides, and accurate returns can only be calculated in arrears on the sale closing date. Interim returns calculated early based on cash flow are unreliable because the biggest inflows tend to occur near the end of an investment and are dependent on the sale value. Therefore, the only accurate calculation is the total compound rate of return from inception through to the close of a private equity transaction. The start year of a PE fund is so crucial to determining outcomes that, like wine, it is referred to as 'the vintage year'. The next milestone for measuring results is the closing date.

Because of this illiquidity, PE firms select businesses with high potential rates of return, starting with a minimum of 25% per year. Meanwhile, overseeing private businesses is time consuming which limits the number of businesses a PE firm can comfortably handle in a fund. This illiquidity and lack of diversity are the main reasons that the potential profit of each business must be sizeable to merit the involvement of a PE firm.

Time constraints are another factor that influences the rate of return estimate. PE funds have a 7-10 year deadline before the fund must be wound up, the assets sold and the money returned to the LPs. There is not a great deal of time between selecting an investment and selling it. A typical holding period for buyouts is 3 years and 5 years for venture. The reason for the different time-frames is because venture companies take longer to mature and to prepare for a sale.

If you calculate $100 compounded at 25% for 3 years, it yields $195, almost double the original investment. Thus PE firms that target buyouts must produce two times their investment. Likewise, $100 compounded over 5 years for venture is $305. This means a venture investment needs to deliver three times its invested capital. This puts various investments into perspective: how many investments can double or triple their capital over such periods? As one GP mused, finding money is not the problem, the problem is finding the right deals.

How do PE firms meet these standards? The primary skill is the ability to select the right deals. In buyouts, winning a deal is more competitive than in venture. Often there is more than one bidder and so a premium to market price, in the range of 15%-30%, may have to be paid by the successful buyer. In good markets, when cash is plentiful, the bidding is aggressive and there is a tendency to overpay. Conversely, a PE firm that overpays is susceptible to diminishing premiums when they attempt to sell businesses, 3-5 years later, if the market is falling.

In venture, the challenge is having the skill to spot a winner, the conviction to take a sizeable position (at least 40% of the equity) and sufficient funds to avoid dilution below 20%. Couple this requirement with hands-on entrepreneurial experience to help steer the company.

During the process of selecting businesses, buyout firms estimate how long they will hold a business, at what price they expect to sell it, how they will restructure it and repay debt.

Because their funds do not "buy and hold" businesses indefinitely, PE firms face a race against time. Based on a 7-10 year deadline; five years can be spent finding investments; three more years spent growing a buyout investment (or five years on venture) and the remaining time negotiating a sale. PE firms need superior discipline and strategic planning to meet this tight schedule and require high potential profits to make it worthwhile.

How PE Firms Measure Profits

There are three measures of profit a PE firm can use to price a purchase and determine an exit strategy: earnings growth, the money multiple, and the leverage (debt).

Earnings growth is the main criterion for judging investments. Growing earnings requires the most skill and exhibits the highest value added to the business. A business that is growing its earnings can make money under many market conditions and is less likely to fall victim to an unfavourable market climate.

Money multiples are important in buyouts and the late stages of venture capital. The money multiple refers to the price paid for a company in relationship to its cash flow. An analogous measurement is commonly used by stock market investors, referred to as a price/earnings ratio. If a company is earning one dollar a share and an investor pays $10 per share, the price/earnings ratio is 10. Since PE firms have greater control over cash flow than stock market investors, they prefer to be guided by money multiples. The money multiple is calculated based on EBITDA, a cash flow calculation that stands for Earnings Before Interest, Taxes, Depreciation and Amortization. EBITDA is a way of comparing the cash flow of different companies in the same business by removing expenses not directly related to operations.

PE firms see EBITDA as a way of comparing apples to apples. The world of private equity revolves around EBITDA. It is the yardstick for buying and planning the exit from businesses. EBITDA is also crucial for optimizing debt levels. The money multiple is simply a ratio that compares the amount a PE firm pays for a business in relationship to EBITDA (or normalized cash flow). For example, if a PE firm buys a business for $10 a share when the EBITDA is $2, the money multiple is 5Xs EBITDA. Profiting from private equity, using money multiple increases or juggling debt, could be a matter of luck. If a company is bought at a low multiple (low premium) and sold at a higher multiple, success comes from buying low and selling high.

The same holds true of debt. If a company is loaded with debt and earnings rise naturally (because of inflation or higher demand) the leverage will propel the profits towards their target because a PE firm has invested a small amount of money to secure a large earnings base. Such transitory opportunities caused by bubbles or strong markets can result in *good timing* being mistaken for *ability*.

Instead of good timing, the best PE firms concentrate on growing earnings. In buyouts, common strategies for growth include selling off mature business units while retaining the dynamic, high growth units. Often businesses are restructured and divisions are spun off so that the company concentrates on its core competence to achieve maximum growth. Buyout firms also employ the opposite tactic. They make a business more efficient by buying several smaller operations and bolting them on to an original acquisition called the platform company. This improves the economies of scale by eliminating overlap and creates a larger, more established brand.

Venture capital companies are disadvantaged by taking longer to mature and having a greater downside. It is also difficult to estimate their future EBITDA. Because 5% of the businesses in a venture capital portfolio produce most of the value, the 'Home Runs' must return several times their invested capital to compensate for the business failures. This is a daunting task. Some PE firms exclude venture from their definition of private equity, only buyout companies could be graced with this designation. Venture is the toughest road.

There are some easy steps a PE firm can take to prepare a business for sale. A quick-and-dirty approach is to cut the operating costs in order to increase the profits. If a PE firm aims for a quick flip this is a short cut to increased cash flow. The downside of cost cutting is that without investing in a company's future, you risk limiting its longer term earnings growth. This is self-destructive if the economy slumps and a short-term investment becomes a long-term hold.

It is difficult to find quick ways to increase the value of a business. Therefore, good PE firms serve an important function: funding new initiatives, creating greater efficiencies, foreseeing opportunities and opening up new markets. At their finest, PE firms are wealth builders.

Nirvana for private equity investors happens when money multiples, leverage, and earnings growth all work in unison at the time a PE firm prepares to exit an investment. However, if only one option is possible, earnings growth is the best choice. Meanwhile the analysis, selection and strategic planning all centers around cash flow calculations, based on EBITDA.

Profitable Points

(Cash Flow: The Lifeblood of Private Equity)

- *Private equity investors depend on a stream of unpredictable cash flow; neither the timing nor amount is predictable.*

- *The only accurate calculation of a fund's profit is the total compound return from inception through to its closing date.*

- *The objective for the annual compound rate of return for a fund is high, starting at 25%. This is due to the greater risks and long illiquidity.*

- *The analysis, selection and strategic planning in private equity centers around cash flow calculations, specifically EBITDA (Earnings Before Interest, Taxes, Depreciation and Amortization). Once the cash flow of a business is determined it becomes the standard for comparing it to similar businesses and for measuring the progress of the business.*

- *The three main criteria for evaluating private equity investments are earnings growth, money multiples and debt structure, all based on cash flow calculations. Of these three, earnings growth is the best measure of success in private equity because it adds the most lasting value to a business.*

55

FOUR WAYS TO INVEST

"Private equity must produce 10% more per year than
a reasonable expectation for public markets; otherwise
why subject yourself to its drawbacks?"

Thomas R. Kennedy, Partner,
Kensington Capital Partners Limited

Private equity captures the investor's imagination. When I was an invest-ment advisor, I received regular inquiries about private deals. Most involved 'Angel Investing', individuals being pitched on start-ups. Many succumbed to the 'family, fools, and friends' circle and lost money. Like fish stories, most had at least one tale of the great deal that got away. Sadly, when it came to pri-vate equity, most investors lacked a protocol for successful investing.

Nevertheless, there is something about private equity that investors relate to. Perhaps public corporations are perceived as overwhelming and impersonal. Public investing seems remote, institutionalized, and more abstract than private investing. Also, the personal connections in private equity inspire trust.

The challenge for investors is obtaining specialist advice and accessing reputable PE firms. The majority of private equity investors are pension funds or institutions, such as insurance companies, endowments and foundations. Nevertheless, there are investment choices for individual investors and there is little reason for individuals to exclude private equity investing. In fact, some advisors recommend 10%-15% in private equity for diversified portfolios.

The reason for the inaccessibility to individuals is that PE firms are com-pact organizations designed mainly to service businesses, not investors. They lack the infrastructure to deal with large numbers of clients. Therefore, they limit the number of clients by the large minimum size of the investment. Many of the most successful PE firms require minimum commitments in excess of $1 million; however, there is a wide range depending on the firm.

I can foresee a future when an infrastructure develops capable of han-dling greater numbers of private equity investors. There are wealth manage-ment divisions at banks and investment dealers that could service more private equity investors. Ultimately, investors who patronize these services will demand greater choice and more alternatives than stock markets alone can provide. To differentiate themselves, wealth managers might offer better access to private equity.

However, wealth managers would need to hire analysts capable of due diligence who could vet PE firms. They would also need protocols that allow investors to properly diversify. When there is sufficient demand and there are specialists capable of advising in this area, then the large minimums that exclude many investors will be reduced.

Despite the current obstacles, if an investor understands the investment choices, it is still possible to find acceptable alternatives. Below are four ways to invest in private equity. All the choices have different degrees of risk and reward and are tailored for different types of investors. If private equity interests you, it is worth knowing how to invest.

Meanwhile, every Canadian now has an indirect participation in private equity through their institutions. Canada's major pension plans (such as Canada Pension Plan, Caisse de dépôt et placement du Québec, Ontario Teachers' Pension Plan) have diversified their portfolios to include private equity. You might feel it is your responsibility to understand how the investments work because you depend on these pensions.

Whether you are interested in finding your own investment path or would like to understand your participation through institutional plans, private equity investing is a fascinating study. I have narrowed the investment discussion to the three typical categories: direct investments, PE funds, and fund of funds. You can also buy the public stock of some PE firms as an indirect way of investing in private equity.

Direct Investment

The most common way to invest in private equity is a direct investment. This means buying a business either on your own or with partners. Buying into a business is an active commitment where investors need a working knowledge of the business or industry and bring their personal expertise to bear. For a silent partner with only a cash commitment, a direct investment still requires on-going monitoring. Except for the three Fs (Family, Fools and Friends), direct investing is only for those with know-how or for seasoned investors.

In Canada, many of our largest pension plans buy businesses directly. The attempted BCE deal is an example of direct investing by the Ontario Teachers' Pension Plan. To protect pensioners' interests, pension plans have representatives sitting on the board and a hand in all major decisions. Direct investing is beyond the scope of this book. It is tantamount to flying a plane solo and requires a separate operating manual.

PE Funds

A more suitable approach for inactive investors involves indirect investing through a PE fund containing investments in several different businesses. These funds combine inactive investors (LPs) who provide capital with active professionals (GPs) who manage the capital and oversee the investments. Such funds are run by PE firms.

Some investors find this partnership arrangement hard to visualize. So here is a simple example: suppose you (LP) have a partner (GP) who you fund while he builds a business. GP receives a 2% annual fee on the capital invested in the business in order to cover costs and to provide him with a base income.

If GP, who is actively engaged in major decisions, is successful, he receives an additional reward when the business is sold. GP receives 20% of the net sale profits called the 'carried interest'. However, before the profit is distributed, LP's money invested in the business must be returned to him and there must be a minimum rate of return to compensate for the use of his capital. This rate is called the 'hurdle'.

For easy math, let's assume LP invests $100 in a business and negotiates a hurdle rate of 8%. A year later the business is sold for $108 after all costs. LP receives $100 back plus the $8 as his hurdle. GP is not entitled to receive the 20% additional reward. However, if the net profit surpasses the hurdle, then the overall split is 80/20 starting from the first dollar of profit. In this case, assume the business is sold for $110. LP receives $108 and GP receives the $2 as his 20% share of net profits.

Similarly, because a PE fund contains several businesses, after each business is sold the GP returns the LPs money in that deal plus the predetermined hurdle and subsequently collects the 20% 'carried interest'.

PE funds typically have a span of 10 years with options to extend for an additional two to three years. Generally after seven years, investors have received all their money back and exceeded the hurdle. The rest of the time is spent winding up, selling remaining investments and making distributions.

GPs have a snappy term to describe the way they are paid. They refer to it as '2 and 20'. Like many concepts in private equity, it is intended to create the same incentive for the GPs and LPs. One Canadian PE firm claimed that almost 77% of their revenue comes from the 20% 'carry'. This has kept them motivated to wring the profits out of their portfolio businesses. The 2% fee keeps the lights on and pays the rent. PE firms should be heavily dependent on the 'carry' for their own success in order to keep their goals in line with investors.

The LP's Cycle

Within the ten years of a PE fund, the experience of an LP is different from that of a shareholder in stock markets. In public markets when an individual decides to invest, the money can be put to work instantly. However, an investor who decides to invest in a PE fund is earmarking a sum of money to invest in future deals. Once the decision is made, the investor signs a legal agreement promising to deliver the money as it is called for. The actual payment of committed funds over time as needed by the fund is called a *drawdown*. If timely payments are not made, the investor is in breach of contract and subject to legal action or to the forfeiture of the investment.

Just as PE firms navigate through three stages: buying businesses, growing and eventually selling them, the investors face a corresponding cycle. The investors' cycle is described as, 'The J Curve'. Like the shape of the letter 'J', initially the value of their investment drops due to expenses involved in buying businesses, covering fees, debt and other on-going expenses. Gradually, in a successful fund, the businesses start to generate returns that exceed the expenses and over time the 'J Curve' loops around and upward. Even successful funds can take 3-4 years to turn positive.

Drawdowns and Distributions

During the early years of a PE fund, LPs are paying in with little to show in return. These payments are the *drawdowns*. Eventually the businesses will provide payouts, called *distributions*. In private equity when the *distributions* surpass the *drawdowns*, the net cash flow is positive and investors start to receive cheques. Usually, distributions start after the 3rd or 4th year of a partnership.

A textbook story of private equity tells of an entrepreneur who sells his business for a handsome sum to a PE firm and retires. The firm suggests he invest some of the cash in other deals they manage through their PE funds. Impressed by their performance, he agrees. The first fund is highly successful, so after a *drawdown* period, *distributions* start as planned and he is rewarded with positive cash flow.

Convinced of his sound judgment, he allocates a significant percentage of his wealth to new PE funds and ratchets up his participation with capital commitments pledged over several years. However, economic conditions deteriorate. *Distributions* stop, but he continues to receive *drawdown* notices from the new PE funds. Desperate, he sells safer liquid investments to shore up his illiquid riskier PE funds. Eventually, a secondary buyer is found to purchase his PE funds at a discount to eliminate *drawdowns* he can no longer afford. This unhappy story is designed to explore some of the concepts of a PE fund. Let's explain the issues and suggest guidelines for a happier ending.

Earlier we talked about cash flow as the life blood of private equity. In stock markets, money stays invested in a corporation as long as the investor chooses. Also, although public corporations tend to pay dividends, they also withhold a proportion of their profits for future growth. In PE funds there is sporadic cash flow as excess revenue is distributed and businesses sold. Investors find it difficult to plan and deal with these unpredictable cash flows.

Hence, investors face three decisions when allocating money to PE funds. The first is deciding on the right amount to invest, because of uncertain distributions. The second is deciding when to invest, since PE firms only fundraise every few years. The third is diversifying; most PE firms only invest in a handful of businesses per fund and have their own niche. Their businesses are limited to certain stages, industries, and geographies. It is important to understand that a given PE fund is usually not well diversified. Here are three pointers for setting up a private equity investment strategy.

Set proper allocations: The first strategy is to decide on the right amounts to invest, so commitments over time are manageable. Most investors under-invest, not taking into account the *distributions*, or over-invest forgetting future *drawdowns*. Finding the right allocation for a PE fund is the trickiest decision.

Diversify your commitments by time: You want to avoid investing all your private equity money at the wrong time in the economic cycle. PE funds are illiquid and you cannot change your mind without penalties. This is the number one consideration for most savvy investors. If you are well diversified-by-time, then the returns of the good years will compensate for disappointing results in unfavourable market cycles. Stagger your commitments across funds raised in different 'vintage' years.

Diversify the types of private equity: You can invest by stages, sectors or geography. The stages could be either venture or buyout investments. You can invest in different sectors like technology, telecommunications, or life sciences. Include different geographies: American, European, and Asian. The diversification should make sense. I heard of a BRIC PE fund that invests in

Brazil, Russia, India and China and wondered how the North American GPs could judge the quality of the legal and accounting information needed to make an informed business purchase.

If all these decisions seem daunting there is a one-stop shopping approach, which brings us to a third way to invest in private equity: fund of funds.

Fund of Funds (FOF)

In the majority of cases, an FOF is the recommended investment vehicle for smaller institutions and individuals. FOFs do not manage nor invest directly in businesses, but rather they diversify among various PE funds. They are skilled in vetting PE firms, fund selection, and at managing inflows and outflows of cash. Whereas PE funds contain only a few businesses and focus on one stage and few industries, FOFs diversify across a range.

Investing wisely in private equity requires more effort than investing in a stock market portfolio. In public equity, there are accepted ways to run an investment program on automatic pilot. For example, investors can buy an index that offers instant diversification, reinvestment privileges and liquidity. The reason public equity is so much easier than private equity is because stock markets can be efficient; meaning that it is difficult for an investment manager in listed public corporations to consistently out-perform the average. Evidence suggests that in public equity the long-term performance difference of top quartile managers is only a few percentage points above the average.[7]

In contrast, in private equity, evidence suggests a persistent performance difference between the top quartile PE firms and the bottom quartile. More startling, this out-performance is consistently better, making it worthwhile to seek out top quartile PE firms. However, top quartile firms are not always fundraising and are oversubscribed. The irony is that the best PE firms don't need more investors. This is where an FOF can be of great benefit. A good FOF has access to the best PE firms in the world.

FOFs spend a large portion of their time screening and selecting PE firms. I interviewed a well regarded Canadian FOF that screened over 1000 PE firms as part of their global review between 2005-2007. They narrowed their choice to 38 firms; most were firms where they had prior investment relationships. Their selection process involved a rigorous formal due diligence process.

---

7. Watson Wyatt Worldwide Pooled Fund Report as of December 31, 2005.

Good FOFs reduce risk through access and allocation to top performing PE funds. Because FOFs create sizeable investment pools with sufficient capital to both diversify among funds and stagger the investment periods, even small institutions and investors are capable of diversifying by stages, sectors, countries and time using FOFs. Meanwhile, they take responsibility for the complicated accounting and reporting of a medley of funds. FOFs offer an easy and efficient way to invest in private equity.

FOFs have another advantage. They are purchasers of secondary offerings which are resales of existing PE funds. This means they negotiate with owners who are disposing of their PE funds. Secondaries are often purchased at a discount to their underlying value and can produce good returns. Because a secondary involves the purchase of a more mature portfolio, you are avoiding some of the downside of the 'J Curve'. Compare it to buying a house that is being built versus buying a blueprint. A new PE fund resembles the purchase of a blueprint. A secondary resembles a house already under construction.

Normally, the vehicle for an FOF is the same investment unit that PE firms use. However, within an FOF, the investor owns a portfolio of PE funds. The minimums can also be much lower. I learned of a Canadian FOF with a minimum of $25,000 per unit.

The major advantage of FOFs is diversification plus the benefit of passive involvement for investors: the chance to "Hire and forget". An important drawback of FOFs is that they add another layer of management fees. FOFs usually charge an additional 1% annual fee on invested capital plus an additional 5% 'carried interest' on the net profits.

Listed PE Firms

Because of the growing awareness and demand for private equity, there are now several well known PE firms listed on public markets. For this book we have interviewed Onex and Clairvest. Both are publicly listed PE firms and their stocks trade on a Canadian exchange. These PE firms went public as early as the 1980s and thus have long-term track records. In contrast, the U.S. has some well known PE firms that have listed only recently on the stock market and have performed poorly. Examples are Blackstone and Fortress Investment Group.

Listed PE firms create a way for investors to participate in private equity through regulated stock markets. they also enable the investor to avoid the long-term commitment of a PE fund. Also, investors can invest as little as they choose based on the number of shares of the PE firm they buy. The disadvantage is that listed stocks, unlike PE funds, move with the stock market. Stocks sometimes trade at more than the underlying value of the PE firm and sometimes less. This can work for or against you when you are buying and selling.

Publicly traded stocks in a PE firm are the easiest way to become immersed in the world of private equity. By understanding the way that PE firms work and their roles as GPs, investors can make better informed stock selections.

Those investors whose imagination is captured by private equity need not feel limited. Once investors understand how private equity works and the investment choices (direct investment, PE funds, FOFs and listed PE stocks), they can begin to explore their options. There is something to fit everyone's portfolio and pocket book.

Profitable Points

(Four Ways to Invest)

- *There are four ways to invest in private equity: through direct investment in a business, by investing in a PE fund or by investing in a fund of funds (FOF). An investor can also invest by buying shares of a PE firm listed on a stock exchange.*

- *The 'J Curve' illustrates the private equity experience in a PE fund. In the early years returns are negative due to management fees, business expenses, and debt repayment. As businesses grow and generate more revenue, investors are rewarded with positive cash flow. This can take 3-4 years.*

- *Drawdowns are payments legally promised to a PE fund by its LPs. These payments must be made as requested by the GP.*

- *Distributions are moneys paid to LPs from profitable investments.*

- *Investing in PE funds involves a disciplined approach which includes knowing how much to allocate, diversifying-by-time and diversifying by types of investments, such as venture or buyout stages, differing industry themes and varying geographies.*

- *Alternatively, an investor can diversify by selecting a suitable FOF. FOFs invest among various PE funds and thus create a diversified private equity portfolio. A good FOF has access to top quartile PE firms not available to ordinary investors.*

- *FOFs deal with all the private equity complexities of selecting managers, proper diversification, investing over time and the complicated administration of multiple PE funds.*

- *Several PE firms have been listed on stock markets. Investors can buy the stocks of these PE firms as an indirect way of investing in private equity without the fear of complexity or long-term commitments. Public stocks can be purchased with small dollar amounts.*

- *Canadian PE firms, such as Onex and Clairvest, have been publicly listed for many years and therefore offer long-term track records.*

- *There is now a way for everyone to participate in private equity, but it is important to understand how private equity investing works in order to make an informed choice.*

SECTION III: THE CANADIAN SCENE

THE STORY OF PRIVATE EQUITY IN CANADA

The New Private Equity Paradigm

Private equity was the original way of doing business. It existed thousands of years ago and continued unimpeded until the 1700s. Businesses were private, small, and managed by the owners. Then as economies progressed, syndicates formed to invest in ever larger enterprises managed by agents. When individual members of a syndicate needed to sell their share of a business, secondary markets arose to accommodate resale.

Eventually, the process was formalized and stock markets with centralized auctions and government regulation developed. As markets evolved and became more efficient the cost of capital dropped and funding business innovation became easier. As a result, when stock markets expanded, they added greatly to a country's growing wealth. This was the direction markets maintained for over 250 years. The ultimate objective of a growing business was to go public. As stock markets became bigger, access became easier for both businesses and investors.

From the 1970s, markets veered from their established course and a new paradigm of private equity took hold alongside stock markets. The new private equity blossomed as a separately managed asset class administered by its own specialists. The key centers for this advance were the United States and the U.K. In order to understand the history of Canadian private equity, we must examine its beginnings in the United States.

In the U.S. during the 1960s astute high net worth investors realized they could turn a tidy profit by buying sleepy public companies and stripping out underperforming assets, such as real estate or poorly managed divisions. After selling these assets and paying down debt, the remaining business generated higher returns and was more valuable. Since high-net-worth investors sat on the boards of universities and other philanthropic endowments, they passed on their approach to the stewards of these worthy institutions. Private equity then became an investment model for the university endowments of Yale and Harvard and resulted in outstanding returns and increased funding for the universities. The U.S. initiative spread to the U.K., which also remains a driving force in this growing field.

65

The pioneers would buy a business that was less than perfect (usually a company listed on the stock market or division of a listed company) and make it more suitable for a sale. The process involved simple financial engineering which meant borrowing against the assets of the business and using the business's cash flow to repay the loan. At the same time, the new owners would sell unprofitable or unnecessary assets and use the cash to pay down the loan.

Private equity brought a new efficiency to the market because listed companies that contained too much fat became takeover targets. Eventually, it became harder to find suitable candidates. Managements of listed companies started to optimize the business assets themselves and sell off unprofitable divisions, rather than risk the sale of their company to private equity and the loss of their jobs. U.S. private equity went through several more developments.

As the U.S. private equity industry matured into the 1980s, institutions set new standards for the businesses they purchased. One in particular pertained to the use of excess capital for acquisitions. Disenchanted with the conglomerate fad of the 1960s and 1970s, institutions were opposed to businesses that made acquisitions outside their area of expertise. This was a profound shift in sentiment because listed companies were accustomed to deciding how to allocate capital and having the final say on the distribution of earned profits. Returning excess capital to LPs, rather than making new acquisitions, became an important feature of PE funds.

During the 1990s, venture capital became the rage, as the high tech revolution gained momentum. Because of easy credit and low interest rates, technology businesses with limited revenue and meager earnings found eager private equity buyers. Easy money meant aggressive bidding and excessive premiums paid for start-up businesses. Successful PE firms depended on good banking relationships and ready access to money, because deals hinged on obtaining the maximum leverage.

The venture capital frenzy ended in 2000 with the bursting of the dotcom bubble and then the focus shifted to buyouts. More PE firms began to concentrate on businesses that could generate cash flow. They targeted companies with a track record of revenues and profits that also had debt capacity. This meant the PE firm could borrow against the assets of the business and depend on business cash flow to cover the debt charges.

With the emphasis shifting to established businesses, private equity continued to grow until its peak in the first half of 2007. When the recovery from the 2008 banking meltdown comes, it is anticipated that private equity will change again. PE firms currently have less access to leverage and will require more skill overseeing and building businesses.

The Canadian Model

In Canada, this private equity model caught on more slowly than in the U.S. because of our unique capital structure and differing needs. In the U.S. stock markets are tightly regulated by a national watchdog, the Securities and Exchange Commission (SEC). In Canada, each province has its own regulator. This creates active competition between the provinces, and the province with the most flexible regulatory environment attracts the most business. Therefore regulations here tend to be more lenient than in the U.S.

A recent example is Enron in the U.S. When the scandal broke, it was easy to impose tough regulations like Sarbanes-Oxley which passed into law quickly. In Canada, because there is no federal regulator, putting rules in place is more difficult. There is less absolutism and arriving at a consensus is unusual. Regulation is a double-edged sword. It improves the efficiency and integrity of stock markets, but it raises costs and inhibits the flexibility of businesses.

U.S. centralized control also increases the incidence of litigation. In the U.S., class action suits have been launched against corporations having a 'bad quarter'. These lawsuits rarely succeed, but they are expensive and distract management.

Because of the more accommodating nature of Canadian stock markets, it is easier to go public, the market is less regulated, and there is not the same culture of litigation. In addition, Canada's lower costs, fewer regulations and lower liability all enhance the decision to go public at an earlier stage. Here, smaller and less developed businesses have access to public capital, whereas in the U.S., businesses delay going public until they are much larger. U.S. ongoing costs for maintaining public listings are more expensive than ours.

Most important, Canada is a cyclical resource-based economy which does not lend itself to private equity. Since our economy and our dollar fluctuate with the prices of resources, our government is supportive of these market anomalies. There is more tolerance of the business environment's cyclical nature. We developed venture exchanges like the Vancouver Exchange and the Toronto Venture Exchange where the threshold for going public is low. We permitted mutual funds to invest in private businesses. Our system is designed to give investors access to private equity-style opportunities through stock markets.

Provincial governments also cooperated by creating tax breaks for investors in small, less mature businesses. Tax incentives like the Quebec Savings Plan and the Labour Sponsored Funds that could compete for private equity financing were offered under the umbrella of stock markets. The list goes on: the popular income trusts were often private equity candidates listed on public exchanges. For all these reasons, the need to develop private equity was not as pressing and the new private equity paradigm caught on more slowly in Canada.

The Hunt for Canadian Capital

In the 1980s when private equity was taking hold in the U.S., Canada did not have enough institutional investors willing to fund private equity type deals. PE firms like Clairvest and Onex went public to obtain financing. This was their only hope of raising sufficient capital. It could be said that Canada was ahead of its time since PE firms in the U.S. have just recently started to go public.

While U.S. private equity started with the endowment funds at universities, in Canada the major thrust came from the banks and pension funds. CIBC was the first Canadian bank to raise a PE fund in the early 1990s. The other big banks followed suit in the mid 1990s. Banks saw private equity as an opportunity to offer additional services and maintain their customer base. By offering private equity to successful business clients, they could nurture their customer relationships from the early lending stage until a potential public offering. This was the ultimate one-stop shopping; their goal was to take a business from cradle to grave.

It was too good to be true. Eventually, the banks spun off their private equity divisions because the model was rife with conflicts of interest. For example, what should a bank do with a business that isn't paying its bank loan when the same bank is also a shareholder?

Moreover, the banks' private equity divisions were doomed to failure because of their flawed business models. Banks are product driven and couldn't resist the temptation to cross-sell products. Owning private equity businesses and putting the bank's capital at risk in order to sell its products at a small profit margin, didn't make sense. Most of the 'Big Five' banks ended up losing money on their PE funds.

Banks turned out to be ineffective business owners. At the time, banks were adept at managing a loan portfolio, but had difficulty enhancing the value of businesses and making them more profitable. In fairness to the Canadian banks, U.S. banks made the same mistake. Banks owning and lending to businesses at the same time created unexpected complications, mistrust and confusion.

There was, however, at least one positive outcome from the banks' foray into private equity. Many of Canada's leading private equity professionals apprenticed and honed their skills at a bank. These individuals then moved on to start independent PE firms. Independence from a sponsoring institution created a superior model. After all, talented professionals did not need the infrastructure of a bank and could build their own PE firms without the constraint of a bank and its bureaucracy. Nevertheless, some of the largest PE firms have been in business only between five to 10 years. I was often surprised at the short histories of some Canadian PE firms with billions of dollars under management despite limited track records.

One managing partner of an M&A firm summed it up for me as follows:

"Private equity in Canada is in its infancy and is the "Wild West" of our financial industry. Public companies have a standardized format for disclosure; this is non-existent in private equity. There is a gap in disclosure and regulation. The bottom line: no liquidity, not regulated, private nature therefore incomplete information, disclosure non existent, sometimes tax driven."[8]

The Canadian Landscape

It is hard to paint an accurate picture of private businesses in Canada because there are no reliable statistics. It is estimated that there are between 30,000 and 50,000 private businesses of any size. Overall, private businesses here are small and if I were to profile their enterprise values (prices at which businesses can be sold), they would line up as follows:

60% are worth between $5 million and $20 million in enterprise value.

30% are worth between $20 million and $50 million in enterprise value.

10% are worth over $50 million in enterprise value.

Private businesses tend to plateau at $50 million, because the market is not large enough for them to expand here and it is difficult to grow outside of Canada. From the perceptive of PE firms, Canada lacks the proliferation of businesses with steady cash flow on which private equity thrives.

---

8. Blair Roblin, Partner, Solaris Capital Advisors Inc.

It is equally difficult to establish the number of PE firms in Canada because they do not need to register. There are anywhere from 150 to 300 PE firms. Most are small with less than $50 million in total to invest, usually run by one or two investment bankers or a wealthy family office.

Of these, about 20 have the resources to manage a fund with more than $50 million in a single PE fund. These are called mid-market PE firms. By contrast mid-market PE firms in the U.S. start with $250 million in a PE fund.

The majority of mid-market PE firms are located in Ontario where Canada's biggest PE deals take place. This is because Canada's major stock market is located in Ontario's biggest city, Toronto. Sophisticated buyouts, where public corporations are privatized, or divisions of public corporations are spun out into private companies, or alternatively private companies go public, all happen in Ontario. In addition, head offices of major banks, investment dealers and accounting firms can be found in Toronto.

Provinces outside of Ontario have developed their own niches. For example, Quebec is entrepreneur-driven and has an active venture capital market. It has the largest number of active start-ups in software, graphics, media, semiconductors and the telecom industry. Quebec institutions back a culture of entrepreneurship with growth capital for information technology, telecoms and life sciences.

Quebec is credited with having the best collaboration between government and the private sector. The Quebec government has fostered private equity through vehicles such as Labour Sponsored Funds which offer tax breaks to investors in private businesses.

Whereas Quebec is the most innovative in starting new enterprises and Ontario with the most sophisticated financiers excels in structuring deals, Canada's best risk takers can be found in the west.

Western Canada is resource based and its economy is built on oil and gas, mining and forestry. There is little or no manufacturing; behind resources, the second major industry is farming. Westerners have learned to live with 'boom and bust' economic cycles and to understand and manage risk. This has shaped their private equity market.

PE firms in Ontario and Quebec avoid resources, but Western Canada's biggest PE firms focus on this sector. ARC Financial Corp. raised $850 million in 2006 in a fund to invest in oil & gas. This is on a par with Canada's biggest private equity investors, such as Teachers', OMERS and Onex.

The resource industry is capital-intensive and high risk. Resources do not produce the cash flow that private equity depends on. Commodity prices are unreliable, which makes leverage or debt precarious. Despite these disadvantages, a very wealthy generation of business people prepared to stake their family fortunes on resources has emerged in the west.

As I interviewed professionals across the country I realized that, more important than Canada's regional differences, is the difference between Canada and the U.S. Many of Canada's PE leaders were educated and worked for top U.S. PE firms or banks. They experienced the contrast between the two countries. The U.S. is very competitive and quick to embrace change where it is feasible. This has given it a leading edge and more growth.

In contrast, Canada is more relationship-oriented. Perhaps this is because the private equity industry is still new and small. Thus, in Canada there is more of a sense of community. Deals are built on close relations, reputations and credibility. Canadian PE firms are less litigious. As one GP put it, "They work with you, not at you." He added, "In U.S. deals, lawsuits are built into the pricing of a business purchase."

Revamping Pensions and Kindling Private Equity

After eighteen months of interviewing private equity professionals and becoming versed in the trials and tribulations of a fledgling industry, there is one story that emerges as a major Canadian success story.

Canada is unique in that we have developed some of the top pension funds in the world, capable of direct investment in private businesses. A few of our public pension funds are able to function as PE firms, buying, overseeing and exiting private businesses. These Canadian pension funds are the biggest direct pension-investors in private equity worldwide. At the same time, these pensions also invest through funds managed by other PE firms.

One pension at the forefront of this development is Ontario Teachers' Pension Plan (Teachers'). Teachers' has one of the best-developed private equity investment units in the world. Between 2001 and 2007, Teachers' alone was responsible for 10% of all private equity deals done in Canada.

It was Teachers' that developed the governance structure that led to the flowering of private equity among Canadian public sector pension plans. The essence of this governance structure (which was copied by Canada Pension Plan) includes a professional board that understands and can manage risk. A

71

professional board is capable of developing a more trusting and innovative relationship with investment managers than a lay board. Also, a professional board is better qualified to monitor managers than lay board members not expert in the financial field. This governance structure was developed by Claude Lamoureux in 1992 when public sector pensions first became active in private equity.

When Mr. Lamoureux was appointed CEO in 1990, all of Teachers' $19 billion in assets was invested in Ontario government bonds. The government had recently established a new independent corporation to replace the Ontario Teachers' Superannuation Fund and to manage the pension funds. At about the same time, the foreign property rule for RRSPs (Registered Retirement Savings Plans) was being removed. This rule had restricted the bulk of pension investment to Canadian property which made no sense for pension recipients because it limited their investment opportunities.

In 1992, as Mr. Lamoureux diversified Teachers' investments, he along with leaders at the Caisse de dépôt et placement du Québec (the Caisse) saw the necessity to invest in private equity. A private equity unit was established and Teachers' started to build up in-house expertise to manage its investment decisions.

As part of this new vision, Jim Leech was hired in 2001 to run Teachers' private equity unit. Under Jim's leadership, Teachers' became one of the world's leading private equity investors. Mr. Leech doubled Teachers' private equity team and is responsible for some of Canada's best-known and most successful private deals.

When Mr. Lamoureux retired in 2007, Teachers' investment performance was outstanding and he left a greatly enlarged pension coffer. Also, Teachers' private equity model had been emulated by other big public sector pensions in Canada. Mr. Leech's ability landed him the job of successor to Mr. Lamoureux as head of Teachers'.

Throughout the 1990s, all the major public sector pension plans went through similar restructurings. These reorganizations were seminal to the advancement of Canadian private equity. Later we describe in detail the reorganization of Canada Pension Plan to illustrate the changes happening in pension management. With the revamping of the pension funds in the mid to late 1990s these big institutions diversified and PE firms sprung up to manage some of their private equity allocations.

There are five major pension plans that PE firms tap regularly for investment capital. They are Canada Pension Plan (CPP), the Caisse, Teachers', Ontario Municipal Employees Retirement System (OMERS), and Public Service Pension Plan (PSP). These pension plans also compete with each other for direct private deals.

When our pensions and PE firms became active in the late 1990s, U.S. PE firms had already started eyeing Canadian businesses, believing there were better deals to be found here. Since the U.S. private equity market was more developed, they viewed our market as offering more room to maneuver and having cheaper business prices.

Although many interesting deals have been consummated in Canada, there are two landmark Canadian mega-deals. They earned Teachers' the respect of Wall Street and recognition for Canadian pension plans as serious private equity investors. Both were engineered by Kohlberg, Kravis Roberts and Co. (KKR), probably the best known American PE firm. Teachers' participated in both deals.

In 1999, KKR bought Shoppers Drug Mart for $2.55 billion in a seven-way bidding war. Shoppers is Canada's biggest drugstore chain. Shoppers subsequently went public in 2001 and KKR sold most of its shares for a handsome profit. Teachers' played a small role here.

The second major deal was the Yellow Pages Income Fund in 2002. This deal put Teachers' on the map because KKR and Teachers' were equal partners. They purchased BCE's directories business for $3 billion. KKR and Teachers' later spun off the Yellow Pages directories into an income trust, called Yellow Pages Income Fund. Again, it was a highly profitable transaction.

The Canadian private equity industry came into its own at the end of the 1990s, so my analysis is based on a five-year review ending in 2006. The significance of this short term analysis is hotly debated and has landed me in some interesting verbal exchanges. But, for our purposes it highlights Canada's challenges and accomplishments. During this brief span, we have created some unique niches: such as world class public pension plans managed by independent boards and a handful of PE firms capable of competing throughout North America. Unfortunately, we can also identify areas that remain under-serviced.

At the best of times there is a lack of diversity in Canadian industry and especially during this five-year period mainstays were disintegrating. Ten years ago PE firms could concentrate on industrials like the auto industry and aircraft parts, packaging, printing, distribution and electronics. This has all changed. Auto parts and aircraft are not healthy industries; packaging has moved to China, printing is hampered by decreased advertising, distribution of major products is handled internationally and most electronics are manufactured off-shore. Economically, the last five years have not been an easy period for Canadian business.

PE firms were restrained by other economic limitations. Canadian manu-facturers were held back by the worry of competition from low cost imports. For a while, the swing in the Canadian dollar from 93 cents to $1.05 and back down made it hard for our manufacturers to estimate their profit margins.

An on-going drawback to Canadian private equity is the relatively small average size of our businesses. Because of their size constraint, the business management does not have the sophistication and depth of their U.S. counter-parts. This makes it difficult to produce the returns required by a PE fund. Therefore, the majority of Canadian small businesses do not qualify for pur-chase by a PE firm.

Most of our big institutional capital is focused on less than 25% of the Canadian economy. Even our largest sales are dwarfed by U.S. standards. A business sale over $100 million is considered a large deal in Canada, but com-mon in the U.S. Our playing field is limited. Therefore, the number of PE firms is small and the businesses they oversee are also small.

For these reasons, the private equity industry has penetrated our economy less than in some other countries. To this day, the private equity industry as a percentage of our gross domestic product (GDP) is lower than that in the U.S. or U.K. and raises concerns that this shortage will constrain the growth of Canadian businesses. Private equity in the U.K. as a percentage of the GDP is double Canada's. According to a U.K. House of Commons Report, 8% of the U.K. workforce is now employed in companies owned by PE firms. This repre-sents about 2.5 million people. I could find no comparable numbers for Canada.

The private equity industry is needed to produce 'growth capital'. This is defined as money required for expansion by Canada's small businesses. Such businesses can be revenue-producing and often profitable, but have a hard time finding money to grow. Because these businesses are in the majority, they rep-resent an important resource. Many could benefit from the support of private equity to take them to the next level.

In addition, because of Canada's history as a venture capital market, the percentage of private equity capital in venture is considered high in relation to buyouts: over a third of our private equity capital is employed in high risk assets which have not produced satisfactory investment returns.

The Canadian Advantage

On the plus side, we have created sophisticated public pension fund investors with sizeable commitments to private equity investing. Our pension plans have the capability to do complex, competitive private equity deals here and abroad.

In addition, in the last five to 10 years, we have witnessed the growth of about a half dozen mid-size Canadian PE firms that are proficient at buying and overseeing businesses anywhere in North America and can compete with U.S. firms. Firms such as these will seed the next generation of Canadian entrepreneurs and create a talent pool to draw on as private equity expands.

The Canadian PE market has a distinctive flavour. It is subdued. We did not have the same aggressive use of leverage and high-profile bankruptcies. Canada did not see the dramatic run-up in multiples or premiums paid for businesses that occurred south of the border. Expectations here were more realistic with less destruction of capital. There is a more collaborative model here.

Overall, I believe the economics of the private equity industry in this country will be rosy once we are past the current recession. It is estimated that over the next five years there will be an accelerating turnover of businesses as the post-world-war-two baby boom generation retires. This is a topic I will return to when I delve into future trends. The available cash to purchase these businesses is estimated to be far less than the available offerings. Therefore the pickings should be good and the prices will be reasonable. This augurs well for PE firms and their investors.

Our private equity industry is unique, requires a local knowledge and hence cannot be easily outsourced. When it comes to Canadian deals over $100 million in size, our PE firms compete with U.S. firms. But the majority of our businesses are below this threshold and, therefore, there will be a demand for home-grown talent. As I interview industry professionals, it is hard not to feel excited about the future of the industry here. Between the rapid rise of our private equity industry and its dynamic future, Canadian private equity is a history in the making.

Profitable Points

(The Story of Private Equity in Canada)

- *The new paradigm of private equity developed in the United States and Great Britain. It started in the 1960s and is therefore over 40 years old.*

- *In the 1960s-1970s the private equity model was straightforward. It started as a way of buying public companies or divisions, selling off unprofitable or unnecessary assets in order to pay down debt and create a better business generating higher returns.*

- *Since its beginning, private equity has evolved and given rise to PE firms that buy both public and private businesses. During the high-tech revolution in the 1990s the focus was on earlier-stage venture capital deals. After the dotcom bubble burst in 2000, revenue generating deals assumed center stage. PE firms proliferated that specialized in buyouts of mature businesses with positive cash flow.*

- *Except for a few early pioneering PE firms, as an industry, private equity developed late in Canada, around 1999.*

- *In Canada, banks and public pension plans were the initial drivers of the private equity industry.*

- *Overall, private businesses here are small and a profile of their enterprise values (prices at which businesses can be sold), would line up as follows:*

  60% are worth $5-$20 million in enterprise value.

  30% are worth $20-$50 million in enterprise value.

  10% are worth over $50 million in enterprise value.

- *A business sale over $100 million in enterprise value is unusual in Canada, but common in the U.S.*

- *During its brief history, Canada created some special in-roads to private equity, such as world class public pension plans managed by independent boards and a few large PE firms capable of competing throughout North America.*

- *Canada's percentage of private equity capital in relationship to GDP is still considered low. Unfortunately, there is a shortage of growth capital, for small businesses under $50 million in enterprise value.*

- *Overall, the economics of the private equity industry in Canada will look rosy once we are past the slowdown. Our businesses are still reasonably priced and a substantial turnover of businesses is expected as the post-world-war-two baby boom generation retires.*

A GOLDEN AGE: 2002-2006

*"On three fronts—funds under management,
investments completed and returns realized—the
industry has achieved a level of success which few
would have predicted even five years ago."*

David Rubenstein,
co-founder Carlyle Group[9]

The five-year period from 2002-2006 may go down in history as a golden age for private equity worldwide. In Canada, buyouts had an eye-popping five-year average annual return of 23.7% vs. 10.7% for the TSX composite index. Money under management in buyouts grew by 82% to $38 billion and overall Canadian money under management in private equity increased by a third to $65 billion.[10]

Some argue this is not surprising since the Canadian private equity industry only became active after 2000. These early acquisitions were cherry-picked. Later, our major institutional investors and high-profile U.S. PE firms became more aggressive buyers of large Canadian businesses, creating demand and thus raising sale prices.

Worldwide private equity also showed very positive returns during this period. The private equity industry became larger, more global and more profitable than at any time during its 40-year history. The quotation above by David Rubenstein from The Economist's 2008 year-end review reflects the generally positive sentiment towards private equity. As shown by Canada's 23.7% annual returns, the appeal of private equity was its potential for impressive performance.

Not only were the returns positive, there was another interesting pattern. From 1996 through 2005, the top quartile buyout funds outperformed the bottom by 15.5% and in venture capital the top quartile outperformed the bottom by 19.8%.[11] A significant percentage of subsequent funds offered by top quartile managers also excelled. In contrast, the top public equity managers outperformed the bottom quartile by a mere 2.7% annually.[12] There appears to

---

9.   David Rubenstein, co-founder of the Carlyle Group, "The Rise and Rise of Private Equity", *The Economist, The World in 2008*, December, 2007, p. 146.

10. *Private Equity Canada 2006, 5 years of Growth*, McKinsey & Company.

11. Watson Wyatt Worldwide Pooled Fund Report as of December 31, 2005.

12. Venture Economics U.S. Cumulative Vintage Year Composite Performance (IRR) as of December 31, 2005.

be a wide dispersion in private equity returns and top PE firms seem capable of repeating good performance. In addition, returns achieved by top quartile funds were difficult to achieve elsewhere.

Professionals ascribe the success to the enhanced efficiency of private equity and the more effective management practices. There is a sentiment within the industry that PE firms create a better business model. The following six attributes are credited with the rise of private equity and its positive performance. These are ideals that propelled the industry in its golden age.

Private equity connects owners and managers through mutual incentives. I have already described the 'alignment of interests' and the fact that active GPs, inactive LPs and key business executives are all expected to put their personal wealth on the line as investors in the businesses they represent. Anyone central to a business's success must share similar downsides and is paid on long-term performance. This fundamental precept is intended to limit the moral hazard of working with other people's money.

Better deployment of capital. Private equity professionals argue that public corporations do not always make the best use of their cash and can be wasteful. At times when leverage would allow a corporation to grow faster, executives of listed companies can be reluctant to take the risk. Also, excess cash is not readily returned to investors and can be deployed to unproductive acquisitions.

Time is measured in years not quarters. Time is used to strategic advantage in private equity. Often public corporations become preoccupied with short term performance. There is tremendous pressure on executives and boards of public companies to show positive quarterly returns. However, sometimes short-term underperformance is necessary to implement strategic changes and adapt to changing circumstances. It is easier for PE firms to make hard decisions because there are no listed price movements to distract them.

Better boards and oversight. Private investors are better represented by their GPs who can play a key role in all important decisions. In public companies, investors and their board representatives can have conflicting needs. Whereas, when a PE firm buys a business its board representatives are themselves investors and are paid on the success of the business. In addition, PE firms tend to get more involved in on-going business governance and strategy to protect investors' interests.

Lower regulatory costs. Compliance and regulatory costs for public corporations have become staggering. Regulation is a two-edged sword. It is necessary to avoid abuse and to protect investors, but it adds significantly to the daily obligations and expenses. Private equity has fewer regulatory hurdles.

Information can be better in private equity. In public corporations, fairness requires that everyone receives material information, such as financial reports, at the same time. Investors and analysts can question the information received but they have no right to gain access to the company's books to verify that it is accurate. In contrast, if a PE firm doubts the accuracy of the financial information, it can send in its own auditor. PE firms can double-check inventory or do environmental analysis. In private equity, it is more difficult for management to massage or misrepresent information.

In practice, principles can be bent and fail when practiced. Nevertheless there is an attitude of committed ownership among private equity professionals. One GP, who preferred to remain anonymous, said that in private equity "we hire five people, work them like ten and compensate them like eight."

Has the new private equity paradigm been sufficiently tested? In Canada, we have not yet seen how they perform through an economic downturn. I heard a saying that I thought apropos here: 'Downturns are to capitalism what hell is to religion.' It is not until things go wrong that we will understand the drawbacks and discover the blind spots in private equity.

There are those who claim that the golden age of private equity was merely a result of low interest rates and easy credit. They argue that the recession will prove that its recent success was a result of high liquidity and will not produce lasting results. As for the growth of private equity investing, some question if the returns will eventually decline towards those of public markets. As the private equity industry becomes more competitive, suitable deals become more expensive, resulting in lower returns. Time will tell if the benefits are meaningful. Later we will explore the dark side of private equity.

Profitable Points

(A Golden Age: 2002-2006)

- *Buyouts in Canada from 2002-2006 had a 23.7% average annual return vs. 10.7% for the TSX composite index. This might be attributed to the fact that the private equity industry became active in Canada after 2000. Hence the deal selection was good.*

- *Worldwide, private equity also did well during this period and became more global, larger and more profitable.*
- *The success of private equity is attributed to enhanced efficiency and more effective management practices.*
- *Fans of private equity argue that it is a better business model for six reasons:*
  - *In private equity, the incentives for owners, managers and investors are more closely correlated.*
  - *Well governed private businesses use their capital more efficiently.*
  - *The timeframe for business success is more realistic in private equity than in stock markets.*
  - *Investors in private equity can be better represented on their boards.*
  - *Agency costs are lower in private equity.*
  - *It is easier to verify company information in private equity than in stock markets.*
- *Overall, the private equity paradigm is still new and untested. Some argue the success can be attributed to low interest rates and easy credit.*
- *It can also be argued that as private equity expands, the returns will decline towards those of listed companies. As demand for private equity increases, the cost of suitable deals becomes more expensive and returns are squeezed.*

CANADA PENSION PLAN: WORLD RENOWNED

"The development of CPP has been remarkable. In 6-7 years, they have established themselves as one of the most important private equity players in the world."

Joncarlo Mark, Senior Portfolio Manager, CalPERS (California Public Employees Retirement System)

One of the most dramatic investment stories in private equity and a testament to Canadians is the creation of the Canada Pension Plan Investment Board (CPPIB). Canada Pension Plan (CPP) is the leader and largest Canadian pension plan. In 2009, it had $116.6 billion in assets, but it is only one of a few cutting-edge Canadian public sector pension plans. The others are Caisse de dépôt et placement du Québec, Teachers', and OMERS. These pension funds are internationally recognized for the sophistication of their investment management.

What makes the CPPIB story impressive is its role in the rejuvenation of CPP against all odds. In the 1990s, it was obvious that workers (stakeholders) were paying into a pension plan where benefits were unsustainable. Once the post-war baby boomers retired, Canada would have a large population of retirees with inadequate incomes because their public pension plan would have inadequate funds to pay them.

Any solution required agreement between parties known for their inability to agree: the federal and provincial governments. The looming shortfall seemed insurmountable. Like similar problems dependent on government cooperation, this issue was destined for a stalemate until the consequences became inevitable. The story of the struggle over Canada's major pension plan is rarely told, but is a worthy contribution to an account of Canadian private equity. The fact that CPP and most of our largest public sector pension plans were reformed ten years ago is unknown to most Canadians.

CPP was created by legislation in 1966 and wholly backed by the federal government. In the 1980s, the federal government suffered persistent large deficits. Canada's credit rating was lowered because of the federal government's struggle with debt and revenue shortages. This resulted in painfully high Canadian interest rates and aggressive federal measures to eliminate the deficit. One source of cheap and ready funding for the government was CPP and other public-sector pension plans, which had reliable, large and guaranteed streams of income from obligatory contributions. As a former investment advisor, I remember the days when CPP was simply a repository for federal and provincial government bonds; many were non-marketable, non-transferable and non-negotiable government securities.

By the 1990s, it was obvious that CPP was underfunded and that there would not be enough money to provide for Canada's future pensioners. Luckily, by this time the government had reduced its debt and no longer needed to borrow from the CPP. Because CPP is a joint federal/provincial responsibility, solving the dilemma of an underfunded pension plan led to endless bickering. Neither side felt the other could be trusted to keep their hands out of the till.

Paradoxically this mutual suspicion had a favourable outcome and the two levels of government established a pension body that was independent of government, but with checks and balances. In 1999, the CPPIB was legislated into existence to manage the CPP. Its goal is to maximize returns without taking undue risk, following clear objectives and tough professional standards.

CPPIB is effectively a multi-strategy asset management firm with three major investment departments: stock market investments, private investments and real estate. Private investments, which include infrastructure and private equity, account for approximately 11.8% of the $116.6 billion in overall assets.

Although CPPIB is a crown corporation, the government does not have exclusive access to information. Also, ministers and members of parliament cannot contact the CPPIB without reporting that they have done so. This makes it difficult for the government to exert undue influence on the organization or its investment selections.

In addition, the charter of the CPPIB cannot be legislatively changed without the agreement of two thirds of the participating Canadian provinces representing two thirds of the population. It might be easier to dissolve the country than to revise our pension plan. (Quebec is not part of the CPP. Instead, Quebec has a pension fund of its own, which is similar to the CPP. The assets of the Quebec pension plan are managed by the Caisse de dépôt et placement du Québec.)

To accomplish CPPIB's objectives without government supervision requires a chain of command, which starts with a board of directors. The board of directors has direct responsibility to the pension plan holders (stakeholders). The board neither represents the management at CPPIB nor the government. In fact, it is the board of directors that hires CPPIB's chief executive officer (CEO) and sets executive compensation.

Board members have no political connections because there is a code of conduct that prohibits political appointments. Board members must have financial, investment and business expertise, and be of the same caliber as leaders at the helm of major corporations, with strong financial and business backgrounds. Terms for board members are limited to a three-year appointment, with a maximum of three three-year terms.

The board's role is to set strategy, review the fund's performance and ensure that risk control policies are adhered to. While CPPIB makes the investment decisions, the board of directors is responsible for the investment policies. Since monitoring and oversight are the main responsibilities of the board, the government has implemented the standards of the Institute of Corporate Directors for best board practices: an independent appointment process free of political conflicts, targeting appropriate professionals and establishing term limits for board members.

In contrast, U.S. pension boards are organs of the state often used to achieve political ends. Many board members have political backgrounds and are not trained in the intricacy of investment management or in monitoring a complex pension organization. Public pension plans across the U.S. have come under regular scrutiny for investment decisions tainted by campaign contributions. This is known as pay-to-play.[13] CPPIB is still in its early days (started in 1999), but I could find no incidence of fraud or graft, leaks or controversial actions.

A serious challenge for an organization that wields CPPIB's control over large sums involves conflicts of interest. Safeguards are built in to prevent this, such as transparency and timeliness of information. The stakeholders of the pension fund are entitled to full, true and plain disclosure, similar to shareholders of a public corporation. Hence, the CPPIB adheres to the same regulations and reporting guidelines as the Toronto Stock Exchange. It has the same accounting mechanisms as publicly traded companies and all information is released to everyone at the same time. There is no insider trading and there are strict procedures that prevent favouritism in making investments or retaining suppliers.

Similar to PE firms, the method for motivating professionals mirrors the private sector. This is intended to align the interests of investment professionals and plan stakeholders to maximize profits. At CPPIB, the compensation of professionals depends on achieving good long-term performance. Senior manag-

---

13. "In State Pension Inquiry, a Scandal Snowballs", NYTimes.com, April 18, 2009.

ers have a variable compensation system where 80%-90% of their pay is dependent on out-performing a benchmark and on risk adjusted returns over a four year period. Professionals are compensated for long-term value creation.

To appreciate our system, we could compare CPPIB to a major American pension such as CalPERS (California Public Employees Retirement System), the world's largest pension plan managing approximately $240 billion in assets. The professionals who manage this pension are civil servants paid on a civil servants' pay scale. Therefore, the compensation does not attract the highest caliber financial professionals. In addition, asset management teams are often understaffed.

Although CPPIB professionals do not have the same financial upside as their peers at a PE firm, they are well paid. CPPIB attracts some of the brightest graduates from top business schools with experience at major financial centers, such as Wall Street, because of the scope of the organization. At the CPPIB, recruits are working for the NHL (National Hockey League) of professional management. The scale of CPPIB deals is in the billions, not millions. Despite its strong Canadian roots, CPPIB is a global player with offices in Hong Hong and London, England. In comparison, no Canadian PE firm has reached this level. CPPIB invests in every asset class so there is a wide array of experience and opportunity.

There are also advantages to working for a public pension organization such as CPPIB in contrast to a PE firm: professionals don't have to raise capital and subject themselves to fundraising every 3-4 years. They also don't face the same volatility. Whereas PE firms could go bankrupt, CPP will always exist.

Internationally, CPPIB is recognized for the farsightedness of its organization, from its well articulated goals to its clear and cogent strategies. Surprisingly, government bodies (federal and provincial) that mistrusted each other succeeded in producing a model that embodied the best management principles and was built to last. If you look at the CPPIB website, you will see that the four-year, annualized return through June 30, 2009 (a very trying time) was 2.28%.[14] Unfortunately, they do not break out the private equity component of this overall return.

In one of the leading management books of our time, "Good to Great",[15] the author describes the attributes that turn a good company into a great one and

---

14. Cppib.ca, Financial Highlights, June 2009.
15. Jim Collins, *Good to Great* (New York: Harper Collins, 2001).

says the following: "When I look over the good-to-great transformations, the one word that keeps coming to mind is consistency." He goes on to describe a flywheel and continues, "However you phrase it the basic idea is the same: Each piece of the system reinforces the other parts of the system to form an integrated whole that is much more powerful than the sum of the parts." This resonated with me, because this is what the framers of CPPIB attempted to do with our premier public pension plan.

ONEX: IN A LEAGUE OF ITS OWN

*"Onex has distinguished itself as a leader in
completing complex transactions. In the case of the
Spirit AeroSystems investment, Onex negotiated a deal
with labour where employees shared in the upside
in return for a more flexible collective agreement.
The transaction took more than a year to complete
but paid off in the end: Onex did well and about
4,700 employees shared $320 million in gains."*

Jeffrey L. Turner, Chief Executive Officer,
Spirit AeroSystems, Inc.

Comparing other Canadian PE firms to Onex is like comparing your corner grocery store to Walmart. With $11 billion of total assets under management, no other Canadian PE firm comes close to Onex. By Canadian standards, firms with over $1 billion of assets are considered large, putting Onex in a league of its own.

Apart from its size, mention Onex to private equity colleagues and there is a note of respect instead of the usual competitive back-biting. This is partly due to Onex' impressive track record of a 29% compound rate of return on invested capital over 25 years; this is noteworthy compared to other metrics or benchmarks. Over a 10 year period the compound annual growth rate on their stock is 7.8% compared to 4.8% on the TSX composite index.[16] Their return has exceeded the top performing North American stock index by at least three fold. Compared to its peers, Onex' performance places it in the top decile of North American PE firms.

Founded by Gerry Schwartz in 1984, Onex has been a public company since 1987. What makes this significant is that Onex was so far ahead of its time. In 1987, private equity was barely understood in Canada and there were virtually no institutional investors in this asset class. This held true throughout the 1990s as PE firms were still rare here. By 1999, when PE firms started to proliferate, Onex was already managing $4 billion.

To this day Canadian private equity lags other mature markets. There are 3,500 PE firms in the U.S., but only a few hundred in Canada. The private equity industry is 10 to 15 years behind the U.S. in its depth and maturity.

---

16. Source: Bloomberg (October 1, 1999 through October 1, 2009).

Nevertheless, from its earliest days Onex had a focus. The goal was to build a world-class business headquartered in Canada. The people at Onex knew they could not accomplish this by limiting themselves to Canadian business opportunities, so they focused on all of North America. Today, with offices in Toronto and New York, Onex owns a portfolio of predominantly U.S.-based companies which in aggregate employs 244,000 people worldwide.

When I met with Andrew Sheiner, managing director at Onex, my goal was to determine what makes Onex unique; was there anything inherently different about the way Onex functioned?

Andrew started by pointing out that, as a corporation, Onex has no debt on its balance sheet. Of the $11 billion of assets under management, approximately $7.3 billion is third-party capital entrusted to the firm by LPs. Based on these sizeable assets under administration, Onex' operating structure is relatively standard and straightforward. The firm is composed of 30 senior investment professionals with a comparable number of tax, finance, accounting and legal professionals.

Onex believes that the cornerstone of the firm's long-term success is its 'culture of ownership'. This culture was established by Gerry Schwartz a quarter century ago, and persists to this day. At Onex, investment professionals are required to make substantial monetary investments in every Onex deal, creating a strong alignment of interests among all stakeholders. Furthermore, when investments are realized and profits generated, up to 25% is set aside to purchase Onex shares in the open market that its investment professionals must hold until retirement. This meaningful commitment, in direct investments and in Onex shares, is reflected in the approximately $3.7 billion of the partners' capital invested in the firm's deals. Collectively, the Onex team owns roughly 30% of the public shares outstanding, so the group shares the consequences of its decisions.

Andrew claimed that many PE firms use only their management fees to fund individual capital investments. In contrast, at Onex, every investment professional must write a cheque, drawn from after-tax earnings, to invest in every deal. This requirement is a guiding principle at Onex and creates a strict and intense investing discipline. When investment professionals sit around the boardroom table thinking "do I want to invest my own money in this situation", it leads to cautious and careful analysis. According to Andrew this ownership culture has served the firm well for many years.

An investment committee composed of the firm's managing directors decides on business deals under consideration. However, because of their personal financial stake, all investment professionals participate in the deliberation, discourse and lively debate.

All of Onex' other investment strategies flow from its ownership culture. For example, Andrew claimed that Onex is conservative about the debt in the businesses it purchases and uses much less than the average industry leverage in its acquisitions, 40% less on average since 2002. From the early 2000s until 2007, when liquidity was flowing and many banks were lending businesses more than they were worth, Onex did not get caught up in the frenzy. When the firm's investment professionals, without exception, are forced to write an after-tax cheque, they think first and foremost about their own exposure to risk.

This prudent outlook drives the price Onex will pay for a business. As a value investor, Onex will not overpay for potential growth. Instead, the team focuses on undervalued businesses at reasonable prices and attempts to grow the business into an industry leader.

A final factor in Onex' success is its hiring practice. There is stiff competition among global PE firms to attract the best and brightest professionals. This can be challenging for a Canadian firm since many candidates have the opportunity to work in major financial centers, such as New York or London. Two thirds of Onex' investment team work out of its headquarters in Toronto, although Onex also maintains an office in New York. Nevertheless, Onex has managed to recruit top graduates from Canadian and American universities with work experience at leading financial firms.

The Onex pitch is that their firm offers the combined benefit of living in Canada (a great place to raise a family) and working with global businesses. Listening to Onex, it sounds enticing; a chance to operate at the highest level of global finance while living and working here. The premise has worked because the professional turnover at Onex is low. Managing directors have worked together on average for 15 years.

At the conclusion, Andrew talked about Onex as a publicly-traded company. Since most investors do not qualify to become LPs in an Onex fund, the public stock is worth noting. He suggested that by becoming Onex shareholders, investors participate in private equity by owning shares in a global PE firm. The public company generates its profits from three sources: (i) the returns on its investments, more than 90% of which are invested in Onex's PE funds, (ii) the management fees paid by LPs; and (iii) a percentage of the carry earned by Onex as the GP.

Through a combination of low leverage and a focus on growing the productivity and profitability of its businesses, Onex has generated superior returns while limiting its loss of capital. This, Onex believes, has allowed it to generate better long-term, risk-adjusted returns. While generating its 29% compound return on invested capital since 1984, Onex has experienced meaningful losses in only three deals and built 60 businesses. Like most PE firms, Onex seeks to generate three times invested capital over a five-year period and has slightly exceeded this average. More important is the consistency with which it has maintained this result for a quarter of a century.

Going forward, Onex has its challenges. The biggest one will be to maintain the culture that allowed it to succeed as its team and capital base continue to grow. The North American private equity industry has become more competitive, mature and commoditized in the past ten years. This causes one to speculate that the easy money has been made and in the future the Onex team will have to work even harder to achieve success.

PART III
THE COLOUR

CONVERSATIONS: THE PRIVATE EQUITY EXPERIENCE

> *"The best private equity firms assume the responsibility
> of ownership. They buy a company, collaborate with
> management, allocate capital, fix problems and set
> strategy. To succeed they must become part of the
> company's fabric or else management will not
> support them."*

James B. Walker, Managing Director,
Callisto Capital

Much of this book is a result of conversations with leaders in Canadian private equity. You can find their names acknowledged at the end of this book. The joy of this book stems from these discussions. Some individuals I met were trailblazers able to articulate their passion and insights in the field. Their interviews provided the knowledge and information needed to write the book. Many conversations were alive with quotations that are used throughout. Meeting cutting edge professionals who built Canadian private equity was the highlight of my experience and I try to express the colour they conveyed.

Eight conversations are covered in detail in Part III to illustrate various niches, while others are woven into the rest of the book. As I interviewed various professionals I explored private equity from different perspectives. There is a wide range of expertise, professional designations, backgrounds, careers, and goals. I used my connections to meet individuals who are respected and of good professional standing, although this book is not a recommendation or endorsement of any firm or person. To ensure that I accurately represented them, each professional had the opportunity to verify their section.

Since Canada had few dedicated private equity professionals until seven or eight years ago, I am impressed with the complex network that has evolved in this short time to service the private equity industry. Despite its brief history, the industry is deep, broad and textured with niche specialties. The conversations selected here provide an overview of the industry.

Not all the conversations were complimentary. The challenges were exposed along with the triumphs. For example, many wealthy investors avoid private equity as an investment option because of the lack of transparency. GPs fundraise before they have selected businesses. These are known as blind pools because investors commit without prior knowledge of the portfolio content. Hence, LPs are completely dependent on the judgment of the GP.

Overall, GPs exercise a great deal of discretion selecting, overseeing and deciding when to sell businesses. Many investors are uncomfortable giving up so much control in a field with few regulations. In contrast to stock markets, private equity exposes investors to greater uncertainty.

This book is titled, *Merchants of Enterprise* because, ideally, PE firms behave like owners buying and selling businesses. They tend to their investments and grow the businesses. However, among some pundits this is debatable. Certain PE firms are perceived as predators and raise the following doubt, "How deeply do PE firms involve themselves in their portfolio companies?" PE firms are neither a substitute nor replacement for management. Rather, PE firms set the strategy and optimize their portfolio companies. If they fail to guide management and play an active role, business problems will not surface until too late.

Thus far, I have presented private equity as an ideal. In "The Controversy" section, I will delve into the downside and describe PE firms that are merely asset managers without adding value. These passive firms act as caretakers instead of visionaries. In contrast, the best PE firms embed themselves in a portfolio company, stress test their financial models and understand the risks. They are proactive and earn the support of management. Superior firms know how to adapt their companies to the constantly changing business climate.

The following interviews took place in Toronto. Although there are many fine PE firms and professionals throughout Canada, Toronto is the hub. All the biggest buyouts occur there. Leading investors are situated there as are specialists in services, such as accounting, legal and consulting. A major accounting firm, attempting to build business, recently placed a specialist in Western Canada. However, there was not enough activity. When a deal was imminent, the parties would say, "Give us the Toronto guy." It was assumed the most experienced people were located in Toronto.

What I enjoyed most while interviewing was the tough individualism. The professionals I met thought outside the box and were not afraid to express their views. They embodied the spirit of private equity itself: stubborn, persistent, and individualistic. Part III chronicles their challenges and investment philosophies. It allows you to see the industry through their eyes and is your guide to the private equity experience.

TWO SOLITUDES: PUBLIC AND PRIVATE

Conversation with Andrew Brenton,
CEO, Turtle Creek Asset Management Inc.

If you saw Andrew at a party, he would quietly blend in; reserved and gentlemanly. Not out to impress. It is when you sit across from him in conversation that you are impressed by his sharp, forceful, dynamic and keen intelligence. From university days, he dreamt of being a full-time investor. Now he has realized that dream, in a company of his own creation, the repository of his hard-earned success.

He talks about his own turning point; a hiking trip with his wife when he worried about the fate of his family should anything happen to him. How would the family finances be handled and who could they trust in his place? It drove him to create a company where his family's future would be protected.

Andrew has mixed views on private equity and can be critical about certain aspects. Hence, he feels he is the wrong person for my project. This captures my imagination so we go on to talk about his background. He worked for a major Canadian bank that asked him to create and then head up their private equity division. As he and his partners started making investments in private businesses he was concerned that listed companies often were cheaper, safer, and had the valuable feature of liquidity.

With this dilemma, Andrew returned to his employer, with a proposal to also pursue opportunities in the public market when it offered better potential. Whereas many professionals in this field are schooled only in private equity, his background in investing in public companies provided a broader perspective. Early on, he developed standards that enabled him to apply the public equity discipline to private companies.

Therefore, his first rule for private equity investing is based on his experience analyzing listed companies. He'd compare a private business to the public equivalents. After checking all the main financial parameters on sales, growth, value and price, he'd only buy the private business if it were cheaper than public alternatives. This rule set the bar for private investing very high.

He describes public markets as ruthlessly driven by frequently quoted prices and the reactions to its constantly changing patterns. These hypnotic fluctuations direct the activity of participants, from company executives to investors, and cast a shadow over their decisions.

"The irony is that daily prices have nothing to do with running a business or its long-term prospects," Andrew says.

"These price changes are often a result of economic or political events; sometimes they are purely technical, such as the selling of a successful position or short covering by large investors. Nevertheless, public companies are often judged on short-term price performance," Andrew argues. The advantage of private equity became clear: there are no quoted prices. Thus, private companies move to a different drummer, evident in the decision-making process of its investors and management.

Investors require a high level of conviction in private equity, because they can't bail out readily. The safety net of a public auction with daily quotes is missing. Therefore, investors can't buy a company with the intention of exiting quickly if they err. Since there is no short-term trading, there is no "greater fool" to salvage them from an imprudent decision.

"This changes the rules of engagement for PE funds," he claims.

PE firms take three to five years to pick their businesses and a similar time period harvesting investments. Each fund starts with an investment in one business and at the peak, portfolios contain only a handful of businesses. "You sink or swim, one investment at a time," Andrew observes. Accordingly, GPs need greater in-depth knowledge of each business they own and a higher level of commitment to its future.

Andrew contrasts this with public markets where funds such as mutual funds are considered remiss if they contain so few investments. "A portfolio with only a handful of companies would be viewed as unprofessional or too risky. We expect public funds to contain a minimum of 50 companies and over the years public mutual funds have become more diversified, holding ever larger numbers of companies."

Public fund managers have less time to analyze each of their many holdings. Success is measured by outperforming an index containing hundreds of stocks, not against positive or negative returns. Public managers are more prone to play the odds and congratulate themselves when they have marginally outperformed a falling index even as their investors lose money. In contrast, PE funds with only a handful of businesses concentrate on good returns and must take a more active role in overseeing a business in order to produce positive performance.

Since GPs can't be judged in the short term, they are compensated for long-term success and receive a performance bonus as high as 20% of the net profit when a business is sold. Their annual fee (approximately 2%) is intended only to pay their operating costs. In contrast, public managers are paid annual fees only, so their incentive is to raise bigger funds with more investments. Since their operating costs are fixed, larger funds mean more fees and greater profit margins.

"Large funds with too many stocks, is this a recipe for mediocrity?" he asks.

Perhaps this is the reason that the best PE funds outperform public equivalents by significant margins. When portfolios are run in a concentrated fashion with few holdings, the performance doesn't revert to the mean (average). Public managers measure themselves against benchmarks containing up to 500 stocks and aim for returns 1%-2% annually above their benchmark. In contrast, GPs at private equity firms are measured and compensated on positive long-term performance. Public managers struggle to beat the average, while top private equity partners differentiate themselves with more consistent and stronger positive returns.

Andrew elaborates, "To earn their lucrative performance bonus, good private equity partners are active in the governance and strategy of the businesses in their portfolios. This results in businesses that are better run. Private equity partners behave more like owners. They impose exacting standards on portfolio businesses."

For example, one of the great advantages of private equity is that businesses are optimally financed. PE funds are driven by the judicious use of cash. Cash does not languish. Debt is employed to the best advantage of shareholders and not for the comfort of management. The opposite can hold true in public companies. While GPs in private equity continually monitor and adjust debt, public executives are not motivated to take on this challenge.

"The tendency in listed companies is to underutilize debt and hold excessive cash," Andrew claims. Public management is hesitant about returning cash to its shareholders. Why should they? Money in the bank is soothing and avoids stressful fund raising when needed. If they exit a division or subsidiary, they don't always distribute the money. Also, they are reluctant to increase dividends when profits are rising. But cash rarely earns an adequate rate of return. So this cushion can cause public companies to under-perform as well as withhold rewards from its shareholders.

"Why don't boards of directors intervene?" I ask.

"Board members are more interested in prudent decisions than in growth. Excess cash can mean less risk. Why put your neck on the block when you could make a mistake?" Andrew replies, "Public company management and the board often support each other."

Debt is a fuel that powers businesses. If you take a business, add a prudent amount of debt (like an athlete on steroids) then the business has the capability to pull ahead, especially with the tailwinds of a thriving economy. Properly used, debt speeds up business growth, pays for research and development and helps a business stay ahead of the competition. However, as anyone with a mortgage will attest, debt means working harder to keep up the payments when business is slow. The downside is increased risk.

In buyouts, PE funds can resort to debt to grow a business and reward investors. Therefore, the success of private equity investing is achieved by profitable businesses using reliable cash flow to handle increased debt with its burden of capital repayment and interest expenses. PE firms sometimes aggressively borrow against business assets to maximize distributions to investors. Andrew calls this active use of debt, "the dirty little secret of private equity." Thus if you adjust for leverage, often the returns of the two entities (public and private) are comparable.

In summary, public mutual fund managers have lots of holdings, own less of any one company, and tend to eschew governance and strategy issues in the companies they choose. They are paid a fixed fee which encourages them to create ever larger funds and dilutes their time with sales and marketing. Their unit holders have no control over the financing of their portfolio companies and thus are not optimally rewarded.

In contrast, GPs have fewer holdings, a larger stake in any particular business, and are paid for performance. To succeed, good private equity managers are involved in governance and strategy for the businesses they hold. In addition, they add value by gauging debt and ensuring that their shareholders receive the benefit of distributions from excess cash or based on increased borrowing within their businesses.

Andrew insists that if public mutual funds were run more like PE funds, their performance would be more consistent. "PE funds," he concludes, "stay focused, dig deeper and add value to the companies under their charge." The alignment of goals between GPs who are paid on positive performance and their LPs is closer than the ties of shareholders to mutual fund managers. Therefore, he is in favour of mutual funds adopting some of the rules that govern PE funds in order to enhance their performance.

PSYCHOLOGY OF A BUSINESS SALE

Conversation with Don McLauchlin, Vice President,
Strategic and Client Development, Roynat Capital

For Don McLauchlin, there is a common misconception that the sale of businesses is rational and dispassionate: two sides negotiate based on objective analysis of a business and its financials. "Nothing is further from the truth," Don points out. "A business sale is high drama fraught with emotion; a cauldron of powerful mixed feelings. To an established business owner, it is a life-altering event. Long after deals are done and calm restored, psychological repercussions linger as suggested by terms, such as 'seller's regret' and 'buyer's remorse'."

Don seems a master of the process. He is a veteran of many deals and has been at the bargaining table on numerous occasions. His responsibility for client development suits his personality. Warm and helpful, he is insightful about the psychological issues affecting entrepreneurs. For investors like Don, being attuned to the mental ramifications of private equity helps his clients keep their perspective. As in the art of war, doing deals depends on understanding the opponent.

The art of the deal will play a greater role over the next decade, as the thousands of baby boomers who built up businesses after World War II start to retire. The pre-war generation grew up during the Depression. They valued work and were not eager to quit secure jobs. In contrast, baby boomers are programmed to retire; their goal is to enjoy the fruits of their hard work. Thus, the process of selling entrepreneur-led businesses is expected to accelerate in the near future and, according to Don, private equity has already become prevalent as a transitioning force in our economy.

That is where my conversation with Don started. We delved into the psychological and emotional subtleties that surround the purchase and sale of a private business.

The Vendor's Perspective

There are always good and bad reasons surrounding a sale. Often the bad reasons are sudden. "Life events can trigger the sale of a business: A crisis such as death, illness or divorce precipitates a sale," Don said.

We alluded to Prime Minister Pierre Trudeau's 'walk in the snow' when he decided it was time to go. Don continued, "Occasionally, business owners wake up and realize that their passion and energy isn't there anymore, or that progress/technology has passed them by."

"Sometimes, owners bite the bullet and act on long-standing concerns. For example, all their eggs are tied up in the business and they are aging. Perhaps the children have left the nest and moved on to careers of their own leaving no one to succeed the owner."

Owners have a tough time wrapping their mind around the sale of a business; some are even pained by the discussion. 'Where will they go? Who will they talk to? What will they do with themselves?' Thus, many of the concerns are soft issues to do with family, ego, self-esteem, and personal fulfillment. Dominant entrepreneurs can no longer be dominant. They started from scratch and touched every aspect of the business—make, sell, ship. Often they succeeded in building large businesses with their drive and hence their identity is tied up in the business.

Guilt can be an inhibiting factor obstructing a sale. "An owner's sense of self-worth can be based on being needed by others," Don explained. "They identify with employees who depend on them or with customers who trust them. They worry about abandoning the people who counted on them. Surprisingly, kids who left long ago to pursue other careers suddenly react when the sale of a family business is imminent, creating further pressure on the owner."

I asked Don, whether this applies to large businesses as well as smaller ones. His answer was a resounding "yes". "I was involved in a company with $500 million in revenue operating in five countries and yet the problems were identical."

I went on to ask about other emotional issues that impact the value and sale of a business. The conversation turned to an owner's relationship to key employees. Don explained, "If an owner wants to optimize the value of his business upon a sale, there must be a management team to replace the owner. A business is far more valuable to outside investors if an owner has trained his successors."

The best entrepreneurs learn to delegate as they grow instead of clinging to old ways and systems. Instead of making decisions under pressure, they gradually establish managers they trust and give them incentives to stay. Don added, "But not all owners are capable of divorcing themselves from past responsibilities. It is important to evolve from a business controlled at the top to a corporation which is a collection of individuals and autonomous units."

Many owners do a poor job of investing in human or organizational structures. Certain owners are control freaks and can't delegate. Sometimes owners of growing businesses are reluctant to delegate functions for fear of dishonesty. Will the employee misappropriate funds or use business secrets to the owner's detriment? Others fear disruption if a key manager leaves. Will it throw their business operations into chaos? Such owners act under duress and make snap decisions in growing businesses, instead of methodically planning. Entrepreneurs are visionaries but not always managers. It takes different skill sets at different phases to grow a business; in Don's words, "different horses for different courses".

Don described the damage that can be done to a business where there is a lack of proper support for the leader. Success can blind owners and push them into jobs they don't enjoy. Sometimes whole operational units grow around an owner that he is forced to oversee. People become ill from years of coping with this lack of fulfillment.

"I worked with an owner worn out from years of managing personnel, overseeing production, creating sales campaigns and dealing with budgets, so he decided to sell his business. However, he agreed to stay on as a salesman. Eventually, he realized that he had found his strength and was experiencing the joy that drove the business in the first place. He asked to buy back in as a minority shareholder. The request was granted and the outcome was win-win."

Surprisingly, the biggest obstacle to a sale is an owner's ego. Nothing seems to threaten business owners more than the suggestion of a management team taking over from them. The gut response is 'I'm not selling'. The reasons for the reaction are complicated. However, the best sales occur when owners can dissociate themselves from their business. They are comfortable and confident and well-positioned to take the next step. They have learned to mitigate their emotion and plan their exit.

"The best business sales are those that have been conceived over long periods, often decades," Don believes. "There are so many elements in planning, but the plan is there on the shelf when the owner is ready."

Don maintained that there are two camps: 'I've got to get my money out' vs. 'legacy and succession planning'. An example is the harm that occurs to an owner in a hurry. Deals take a long time to complete. Employees watch and worry about losing their jobs. They start to prepare resumes. Key employees need to be retained by reassuring them through the critical negotiating period. Without their support, the value of the business erodes.

Don's parting advice for business sellers, "Get out when the going is good. The best time to sell is when the financial cycle is favourable, earnings are good and the industry is doing well. It is easy to structure a sale."

"However, this advice is counter-intuitive", Don admitted. "Most people do the opposite, they coast until things are tough. Then they are forced to struggle with a challenging environment and few buyers." If calamity strikes, unless the owner has amassed sufficient cash outside of the business, the options for a business sale are limited.

"If you are a business owner, you must accumulate wealth outside of the business, learn to delegate and make your own job redundant, have an exit plan on the shelf years in advance, and then sell when everything looks perfect."

The Buyer's Perspective

Don had equally strong views about buyers. "Understanding the mindset of the vendor helps buyers make better-informed decisions. I do not believe in paying for success, because it involves buying at the top. I am a fan of buying businesses which are selling at a discount to the market. Often, these are underappreciated businesses; they may be for sale at the wrong time in the business cycle, or in a misunderstood industry; perhaps they have a fixable problem."

Don cited an adage that says, "find out before you get involved because you will learn three times as much once you own the business."

Along the same line, he is in favour of business purchases where the buyer is back-stopped by the vendor. In other words, the seller stays involved by owning a percentage of shares or lending unsecured capital to the purchaser. Unlike some buyers who insist on control of a company, Don does not. He can be tempted to buy a minority share.

"A successful business owner can become like a deer in the headlights, frozen by the fear of risk-taking and unable to progress. Sometimes a minority buyer provides the reassurance that there is an investor backing the owner with skills and deeper pockets. Thus, the minority investor liberates the owner by allowing him to remove some money and frees him from the fear of making big decisions. An owner who felt trapped by the wealth accumulated in his business is no longer hampered by an overly cautious stance and can take the business to the next stage. Such a minority purchaser needs to be protected through a shareholders agreement, but minority ownership in these situations can be very attractive."

101

"Apart from price where do you want to hunt?" Don continued. "Invest in what you understand. Have a checklist of good industry fundamentals. Then decide what makes a business appealing. Is the business in a niche or is it an industry leader?"

When I left our meeting, I felt I understood the importance of psychology in a private equity deal. You must assess the psychological strengths and weaknesses of the individuals involved. At one point, Don mused that the best vendors were the "planning types". I conclude that the same holds true of buyers.

PREPARING A BUSINESS FOR SALE

> Conversation with Jeff Pocock and Blair Roblin,
> Partners, Solaris Capital Advisors Inc.

Having grasped the emotional turmoil surrounding the decision to sell a business, I wonder how this impacts the process of preparing a business for sale. I turned to the firms that act as intermediaries between buyers and sellers and have the responsibility of closing a sale, the M&A firms. Normally, M&A firms are hired by and represent the seller. Their role in the drama is replete with secrecy and intrigue.

I went to an independent M&A firm that concentrates on small to mid-size businesses ($20 to $100 million in enterprise value) and specializes in business sales, Solaris Capital Advisors Inc., where I met with two of their partners. They are solid professionals with impressive credentials and long-term experience. Blair Roblin, a lawyer and MBA, previously worked for large, high profile accounting firms. His partner, Jeff Pocock, a C.A. and MBA, has an equally substantial background. We started by discussing their preliminary meeting with an owner thinking about selling.

Invariably an owners' first question is: "How long will it take to prepare the sale and who will find out?" Confidentiality is a major consideration in a sale. The transaction must be hushed up until an appropriate time or the competition will pounce. A business sale presents an opportunity for the competition to improve their relative standing.

We discussed the secrecy issue further. "Select employees need to know earlier than the rest or it will create widespread uncertainty, " Jeff suggested. "For example, senior sales people need to know or else there is a risk that they will find out from competitors or colleagues."

"The preparation process starts with an estimation of the price, and the owner is asked to compile the information needed by the advisor," Jeff pointed out. "It is surprising how often the owners don't have the data. The financial information generally resides with the chief financial officer or controller, but the owner doesn't necessarily want to inform them of a potential sale.

However, even after the information is received, its caliber is often questionable. Most small business financial reporting is tax-driven, where highlighting business success is not the goal. Therefore, the information must be restated to remove items like shareholder bonuses or depreciation that is accurate for tax purposes, but does not reflect the business potential. A major role of an M&A advisor is getting the right information and putting it in a reliable form to accurately reflect the business value. Buyers also need a business plan in order to understand the potential of the business they are being offered.

"In twenty years, I have never met a client that has a five-year business plan." Jeff said.

This leads to a discussion of the often dysfunctional nature of small businesses. Businesses confuse a one-year budget with a business plan. Budgets are necessary and useful to control spending but they do not offer a vision.

"The business plan is central to a sales process," Jeff explained. "It outlines the history of the business, its geography, sales, and where the concentration of sales exists. Buyers want to know what the business has to offer. Is it a valued brand, does it have leading-edge technology or innovative business systems? The business plan needs to outline new products, customers, the macro-economics of the industry and where growth will lie. While the plan must be in marketable terms, it must also be defensible."

A distinguishing difference between small businesses and big businesses is the existence of a five-year plan. In big business, such a plan is a feature of their operations and an on-going document. Sometimes referred to as a living-document, it keeps the business focused on growth opportunities. However, small businesses only do extensive preparation at the time of a sale and the information is compiled in a sales document called an Information Memorandum.

Solaris sent me home with a checklist which covers all the complexities involved in producing a long-range plan and I now understand why smaller businesses do not have the personnel or skill to maintain one.

Inadvertently I asked, "Are you dressing up a business for sale?"

Jeff winced. Perhaps he sees my question as trivializing his role and perceiving his job as mere window dressing.

He explained: "It often takes a year to make a company more marketable. During that time we are doing our own due diligence on the company, coordinating with the accountant and lawyer." He described the involved risk assessment. "What is the depth of management? Are there qualified subordinates capable of taking over? How about the sustainability of the business?"

"Is this a one-trick pony?" Jeff added, "In other words, does the business have one product in one geography?"

A good business plan describes both the advantages of a business and its drawbacks. If a vendor is not forthright about risks, purchasers pursuing their own investigation could refuse to close. Jeff continued by describing common risks: "Is the company capital intensive?" Meaning, will it take a lot of money to stay competitive. "Who are they dependent on? For example, do they depend on one customer or one supplier who could disappear?"

Their shortest deal took four months to prepare, but eight to twelve months is more common. However, their closure rate is high because they wouldn't take on a risky mandate. Solaris is not paid unless the business is ultimately sold. This means they can work for a long stretch, assessing a company, advising and solving problems, but receive no pay if there is no sale. It sounds nerve-wracking to me. To protect themselves, they only work with businesses in which they have confidence. Taking on a business shows conviction on their part and is like a seal of approval.

Since they are investing their valuable professional time in the process, I asked them how they size up management teams for the businesses before they take them on. Jeff replied: "Firstly, businesses we work with come recommended by known professionals, like accountants, lawyers and bankers, who have worked with the management and have an inside track."

"Secondly, we do our own homework and meet with every member of the executive team to assess their capability. We favour businesses where the management has been running the business for many years and the managers' experience and character show." I gather that too much turnover creates suspicion. Armed with the management's backgrounds, they move on to analyze the enthusiasm, vision and strategy of these executives.

"We are aware of the fact that owner-operated businesses have a tendency to hire based on nepotism," Jeff pointed out. "But family members or friends may not be the best managers for the business. A business that has limped along because of a son or son-in-law, not chosen on merit, must now be repaired." This is one of the dysfunctional qualities of small business that M&A firms are equipped to deal with. Replacing family or friends is a task best left to an outsider, such as an M&A firm.

Once they have a presentable management team, they work with them to formulate a business plan. Blair added, "We ask management, if money is no object, where would you like the business to go in the next five years? When they come to us, hopefully, they have thought this through and can present a reasonable proposal. We go back and comb the numbers looking for confirmation through past performance. If there is weakness in the numbers it is easy to pick up."

Jeff added, "Of course, expectations of purchase price need to be reasonable."

"Our best owners are looking to *double dip*," Jeff continued.

He explained that many owners are not looking to completely retire from their business. Owners interested in seeing the business grow are looking for two big liquidity events. "At some point, owners feel they are too exposed if all their cash is tied up in their business. They turn to M&A advisors to cash out of a portion of their business. Often the owners have experience and energy. Therefore, they maintain 20%-50% with an eye towards growing the business. Down the road (around five years later), they have an opportunity for another big pay day. This is referred to as, *double dipping*; being paid for the same business more than once, as it continues growing."

I summarized the major points leading up to the sale: the need for secrecy, the complex review process, the assessment of a business and its industry, the realization of business deficiencies and the overhaul of aspects unacceptable to buyers. Then comes the actual sale. An M&A firm's preferred method of selling a business is through an auction. Often PE firms are bidders at these auctions.

Unlike ordinary auctions, filled with hype and mass marketing, in a business auction the M&A firm canvasses perhaps 50 potential buyers. The number varies depending on the mandate, but can reach 100 prospects. If some show interest and meet the qualification standards then they receive the Information Memorandum and they go through a screening process. Potential buyers have a month to show expressions of interest and can take several months after that to do their own due diligence.

Credible buyers are introduced to management and are put on a short list. My obvious question was, "How do you avoid the competition learning trade secrets?"

Jeff and Blair claimed that information is only released in stages as buyers become more serious. Sensitive information (such as trade secrets, patents, customer lists and price lists) is released last. "The competition doesn't find out until they have spent a lot of money on due diligence. Their expense grows as the process grows."

I would imagine, at this stage, the owners can choose with whom to negotiate but there is no way to completely avoid disclosure to the competition. There are advantages and disadvantages with selling to either competitors (strategic buyers) or investors (financial buyers). Competitors are interested in the synergies of a merger and acquiring customers and can tolerate operational flaws. In contrast, for investors the depth of existing management is critical.

Having worked in an investment firm owned by a major bank, which contained a large M&A department, I wondered about the advantage to a business owner in working with a small M&A firm, like Solaris. I posed this question to Jeff and Blair.

Jeff and Blair worked for both investment banks and major accounting firms, which contained M&A divisions.

Blair offered an explanation, "Both investment banks and big accounting firms cross-sell products. Both have different services with different revenue streams; they are advisors plus product providers at the same time. Therefore the advice can be conflicting."

They ended by emphasizing that they are independent, that the majority of their revenue comes from selling businesses and that they are only paid if a business is sold. Solaris is a good example of a local M&A firm with a single purpose. The majority of their deals are located in Southwest Ontario. Since selling private businesses is a very discreet process, the regional nature of this M&A firm allows them to know the credible buyers.

As opposed to Solaris, M&A divisions at major accounting firms and banks tend to be involved in deals over $100 million in enterprise value which require more specialists and resources. Businesses that gravitate to the major firms are more complex or involve a wider territory. Majors also have a potential clientele of business owners where they have done the on-going accounting work or financing and know the businesses well. Lastly, M&A firms at large investment dealers specialize in taking a business public.

M&A firms, small and large, play a vital role in business sales. They are important to the smooth performance of the Canadian private equity industry.

THE POWER OF INCENTIVES

Conversation with Jeff Parr,
Co-CEO and Managing Director, Clairvest

Started in 1987, Clairvest is one of the original Canadian PE firms listed on the Toronto Stock Exchange (TSX). Currently with $600 million in assets under management, it continues to be one of a few Canadian public firms of this kind. I met with Jeff Parr, Co-CEO and Managing Director, to gain insights gleaned from their long-term experience. Within the first few minutes of our conversation, he opened with one of Clairvest's guiding principles.

"When we invest in a company, the CEO of that company has to have a sizeable ownership position in the business. We augment this ownership with related incentives. However, if the CEO doesn't have significant downside, we won't participate."

He backed his statement by referring to a 2006 report on private equity compiled by Ernst and Young (E&Y). I hunted down the report which sets out the drivers of value in private equity.[17] E&Y calculated returns on 103 businesses; a combination of both European and U.S. businesses sold in 2006. They interviewed PE firms responsible for 81 of the deals. Their combined U.S./European sample achieved an average total investment return of 63% for all businesses sold in that year. The average holding period was 3.5 years.

One conclusion of the E&Y report was of particular relevance to our conversation: Selecting the right management team and aligning objectives are key to the success of a deal.

In both Europe and the U.S., private equity outperformed public company benchmarks on most of the metrics used by E&Y for evaluating business success: Enterprise value, EBITDA and employee growth. Although they offered several reasons for this, the most pertinent was ownership by management.

This same premise guides Clairvest when they invest in businesses. They aim to partner with a good management team and invest alongside them. When Clairvest negotiates a purchase, previous owners are offered as much as 30%-40% ownership of the new company. Unlike PE firms that insist on majority ownership, Clairvest is also comfortable with the purchase of a minority interest and permitting existing management to retain control. If previous

---

17. *How do Private Equity Investors create value? Findings from Research of US and European Exits in 2006*, Ernst and Young, Private Equity Services.

owners aren't prepared to risk a significant amount of their personal capital, it is usually an unfavourable omen.

"If you are counting on vendors who ran the business but won't make a financial commitment, you have no glue to hold your operation together," Jeff pointed out. "Previous owners are offered a minimum and maximum participation in Clairvest's new endeavor. When they opt for the maximum ownership that is a great sign."

"What the E&Y article shows is that fiduciary obligations towards the business, bonuses or option plans don't produce the best results. Rather, success comes when the executive officers have ownership in their business, together with the PE fund."

Although ownership can be made easier with interest-free loans, advantageous payment schedules, and favourable pricing to make management's commitment less onerous, people should not be relieved of their obligation. Employees don't try harder when their options are under water. Incentive plans can't be all upside.

Jeff is a fan of all key people putting hard cash in a deal. "Options and other means of retaining or motivating people are insufficient to properly align management with Clairvest's PE fund. The problem with incentive plans alone is that they offer no downside."

"With options, people stay on until the business gets stuck. If people have money in a deal, it keeps them working through the hard times. Leaving is painful."

"You don't need more partners when things are going well."

According to Jeff, staying power is the key to success; you must be able to survive capital market and debt volatility. When Clairvest invests in a business, it might be at the wrong time in the business cycle, interest rates might be high, but keeping the team together despite adversity is a business-building strategy. It maintains discipline through adverse circumstances when Clairvest may have overpaid or faces higher interest rates or an economic downturn.

Clairvest has a carefully formulated system for identifying and rewarding key people. The first incentives are to owners vital to the future of the business. These people are then asked to compile a list of strategically important employees who are offered an opportunity to invest in keeping with their position. It is made clear that they are part of a select group being offered ownership.

Jeff added that the pitch is simple: "You are an owner and we will help you, but you must be part of the team. If refused, the fact that a person doesn't want to be on the team says something. They become an employee and no longer a member of the A team. If you don't invest, you are not committed."

I asked about the problems with this alignment of interests, "What if you want to change the CEO who now has a significant ownership in the business?"

Jeff was prepared for this question, "This is not an uncommon problem. CEOs who built a business are used to having complete authority and need to be transitioned from unchallenged leader to team captain."

I am reminded of a clever comment by another interviewee, "Own the company, don't be the company." But, what happens when a CEO is not emotionally capable of making the change?

"This is another place where alignment of interests is beneficial." Jeff said, "You want a CEO who cares more about his capital than his job. Hopefully, the bias of a CEO who owns a significant portion of a business is to protect his investment rather than hanging on to the job." There have been times when Clairvest needed to replace the CEO. The CEO maintained his ownership, stayed on as a board member, but was no longer part of the executive team.

Jeff gave another example of alignment of interests and how Clairvest best serves its LPs. Where Clairvest acts as the GP, it owns a minimum of 25% of each investment so that Clairvest's corporate capital is invested alongside the LPs.

I pressed Jeff for additional insights into how Clairvest operates and soon our conversation focuses on other key policies.

Jeff believes in concentrating capital into businesses and industries that they know well. "We never manage more than three businesses per Clairvest professional. Clairvest has a strong financial orientation and focuses on the best use of our financial skills." He went on to explain, "Most of the businesses we invest in require upgrades to its internal systems, so we concentrate on the rigour of our own in-house reporting tools. We maintain aggressive metrics for comparable businesses, which forces accountability on the business management team. There is no place to hide."

Maintaining active involvement at the board is important in Clairvest's drive to add value. This is done in two ways. First, Clairvest partners sit on the board. Secondly, the board is built for business enhancement. In addition to the business's own executives, the board includes seasoned industry experts selected in keeping with the growth strategy for a particular business.

Jeff returned to the theme which launched our conversation and explained the incentives for partners working at the firm. "Since Clairvest is a publicly traded corporation, partners are expected to invest a significant portion of their own capital in the firm's public stock."

This policy is designed to align the partners' interests with Clairvest, so that they make better risk-adjusted decisions. Clairvest professionals own 60% of the public corporation and its board of directors owns 20%. This means that the lion's share of the stock is owned by Clairvest principals. This fosters a strong team and long-term commitment to the corporation and its shareholders. The remaining 20% is owned by the general public and trades on the TSX.

Jeff claimed that Clairvest stock is often a cheaper alternative for retail investors who would like to invest in private equity and do not qualify to become LPs. Generally, the stock trades at a discount to its break up. In other words, you are buying the private equity businesses in Clairvest at less than Clairvest's book value.

He proudly referred me to their public financial statements which have been designed for transparency and clarity. However, he is careful to caution me about the long-term nature of the stock. "Any investment in private equity normally takes 10 years to come to fruition. Therefore, investors who buy the stock need a long-term horizon."

Clairvest reported a 9.5% compound annual growth rate for the past ten years on their stock (from October 1, 1999) compared to the ten year compound annual growth rate for the TSX composite index of 4.8%.[18] The performance was worth the wait.

---

18. Source: Bloomberg (October 1, 1999 through October 1, 2009).

THE ERA OF RETIRING BABY BOOMERS

Conversation with Elmer Kim, Managing Director,
Whitecastle Private Equity Partners

In the chapter on the Canada Pension Plan Investment Board, I touched on the ageing of the post-world-war-two baby boomers. This massive demographic shift has powerful implications for the Canadian economy, and was the cornerstone of my conversation with Elmer Kim of Whitecastle. We talked about the forthcoming transformation in Canadian business as the baby boom generation retires and sells businesses built over 30-40 years. These businesses must transition in order to generate liquidity for their owners, train the next leadership team, maintain employment and offer continuity of goods and services.

Many owners already face tough times. The economy has slowed; globalization threatens and manufacturing is shifting as mainstay industries, like the auto industry, disappear. With advancing age, many baby boomers lose their appetite for risk and no longer want to expand. This could result in stagnation or decline of their businesses. Economically, this has serious consequences for Canada.

Elmer claims that the advisors and the support system for this small business transition, as baby boomers sell their businesses, is not yet in place. "Institutional investors, banks and major accounting firms in Canada favour big deals. Thus, small businesses fall through the cracks," he said. "Canadian private equity is 10-15 years behind the U.S. There are not enough PE firms with track records that can raise capital in order to transition and grow small businesses."

For these reasons, Whitecastle feels this is the area where it can add value. It targets small businesses that lie at the heart of the Canadian economy and are in the majority. Whitecastle buys businesses that are less than $75 million in enterprise value and have cash flow (EBITDA) of $2-$10 million. Elmer feels this area is inadequately serviced and that access to capital will be a constant concern. "For big businesses money has been chasing deals; but for small businesses it is hard to attract capital," Elmer explained.

"The lack of interest in small business is not surprising since this niche involves higher risk and requires more work," he continued. "Businesses in this range are usually run by a founder and one key manager. They generally function on an ad hoc basis without middle management or state of the art accounting and information systems. They lack solid business structures, management talent, and a hierarchy."

Whereas large businesses have systems and people in place, in a small business the control panel usually resides in the owners' head. The first priority is to enhance management so that the founder has more available time and support. The founder had several decades to learn the ropes, but for new owners overhauling a small business is time consuming and costly. The business might require revamping and expensive consultants. Integrating new people and ideas into an old established business changes the culture and dynamics while on-looking competitors, aware of glitches and the changing of the guard, have an opportunity to lure away customers.

"There is a serious lack of mid-management superstars, which has restricted the scale and scope of many businesses," according to Elmer.

Whitecastle operates in Southern Ontario, Quebec and Alberta. It shops for growing businesses with a local flavour and avoids businesses where it must find customers or relocate a plant. However, the industry choice comes first.

"When an industry is growing, management can't do anything wrong; when the industry is suffering, management can't do anything right."

Whitecastle's partners feel they are active participants in future business growth. Having looked at many fund websites, I challenge this saying every fund company makes the same claim. It is my understanding that the majority of PE firms are peopled by financial types and lack the proper diversity of management talent to grow a business. Most partners at PE firms are good at valuing a business, but have never actually managed a business.

Elmer explained that big mature businesses can coast for awhile. However, because of the junior nature of the businesses in its portfolio, Whitecastle doesn't have that luxury. Whitecastle won't invest in a business without having in-house experience in that sector to depend on; it relies on its network to understand the issues. Over the years, it has developed a good group of operational people who can take a business to the next level.

"In the past, some fund companies could profit through financial engineering alone, such as reducing costs or selling assets, but this is no longer the case," he adds. "Whitecastle has a high ratio of managers to portfolio businesses in our talent pool. Active participation is essential for survival and to enable a profitable exit strategy in small business. Rarely will we invest if there is no path to new management." To increase the odds of finding the right management, Whitecastle uses two strategies.

"Firstly, Whitecastle cultivates a circle of senior management that we can marry into a new business; many have run large institutions or corporations. When we consider a purchase, we ask members of our circle if they are prepared to become full-time managers in a particular business."

Secondly, Whitecastle has an 'Executives in Residence' program to take advantage of strong executive talent. Together, Whitecastle and the executives search for business opportunities suited to the executive's expertise where they can partner together.

"We won't invest if we can't count on this type of talent. This executive stays with a company often for two and a half years until Whitecastle can transition to the next CEO."

"We have a saying at Whitecastle," Elmer explained, "We wouldn't buy a car without a driver. Whitecastle will inject capital if we have the assurance that previous management will stay for a given period. Then we work with young immature management groups where we must nurture the culture and develop a functioning team with efficient operating systems. We often start from scratch and implement processes, a chain of control and bottom line accountability"

Meanwhile, the old management stays and continues to have a meaningful stake in the business. However, proven management (such as the 'Executives in Residence') is critical and works in parallel with the existing management. These 'Executives in Residence' invest capital up front and at the same cost as Whitecastle. For everyone to pull together, risk is spread among the old owner-managers, Whitecastle and the new executives. Any in-coming CEO must have a sizeable portion of his net worth in the business (usually this excludes the family home). In return, new management has a significant chance to increase their personal net worth.

When Elmer finished his description of transitioning from the old to the new, I understood how precarious it is taking a small Canadian business and transitioning it to new owners. I realized why more PE firms have not stepped up to this plate. Two complex feats must occur simultaneously for a PE firm to succeed. Moving a business to new owners is high risk in its own right, but concurrently the business must grow significantly to justify the new addition of investor's cash. PE firms consider 25% to be the potential annual rate of return needed to justify the high risk.

I wondered how Whitecastle could possibly add value under these circumstances and we moved to a discussion of how businesses grow and the role of Whitecastle. An established business can grow in one of two ways. Firstly, it can grow organically, by developing new products, divisions or lines. "A company can sell more to the same customers or sell the same to more customers."… or both!

The second road to growth is through acquisitions. Larger businesses in an industry sell at greater premiums. Smaller operators in the same field sell at lower premiums, sometimes at less than half the price. Professionals can purchase small operators and bolt them together to create more valuable players. This strategy drives the combined entity to the premium price of a large business. Whitecastle is capable of buying a small successful business and using it as the base or 'platform'. Once the 'platform' is operating smoothly, Whitecastle buys small complimentary add-on businesses to expand its platform business.

Elmer explained 'platforms' and growth by acquisitions. "The first investment in an industry is the riskiest. This is called the 'platform' because we must buy a business, build a vision and infrastructure. Once the business is functioning and profit margins are reasonable, the major hard work is behind us. Whitecastle is no longer dependent on changing the management; the strategic relationships are in place."

He continued, "With a successful platform, we become an industry insider and can maneuver using our experience. Buying the next small business in the same industry increases our market share. Now the goal is to reduce overhead and increase the scale and scope of a business by integrating the two purchases. This process can continue with numerous acquisitions." Whitecastle invests mainly in Canada, but it does venture outside if the platform business can use its expertise to purchase a U.S. subsidiary.

He gave me an example of an environmental company in the traditional garbage collection industry with which they are working. "As an industry, earnings were stable but not growing. The industry was fragmented and needed consolidation. By improving the services to the customer, our company could grow faster than the competition and earn higher profits. Whitecastle's research showed that recycling was gaining importance while profit margins in garbage collection were dropping. The challenge was to help customers recycle more and throw out less. We refocused the business into recycling and then used it as a base to purchase other operators and grow."

Whitecastle looks at 150-200 deals a year in order to find a few suitable choices. Elmer said there is no shortage of small business opportunities. His problem, as well as that of his competitors, is deal flow and getting the pick of the litter. He welcomes competition, because he feels it generates more activity and is good for all the PE firms.

What makes the coming transition in the Canadian economy so attractive is that the economics of the industry favour the PE firms. The estimate of businesses for sale is in the billions of dollars, but the amount of money available for purchases is a small fraction of that. Therefore, the pickings will be good and the prices should be reasonable. For Canada's small businesses, it will be a buyer's market. Canada needs to create, build and encourage talent in the private equity industry. The first baby boomers turn 65 in 2011.

DATABASE FINANCING

Conversation with Leon Raubenheimer,
Managing Partner, ZED Financial Partners

As I became aware of the predictions of cash shortages for baby boomers selling their lifelong businesses, I explored different private financing alternatives. One of the firms with a unique approach is ZED Financial Partners, where I met Leon Raubenheimer, managing partner.

Leon's approach to private equity stems from his background as a South African banker, combining debt and equity financing. His firm focuses on the skillful financing of businesses but, unlike M&A firms, does not give advice. If his firm succeeds in financing a business, ZED is paid a finders fee.

We start by discussing the harshness of the Canadian business environment compared to our Southern neighbours. Not only are private businesses small, but 70% of them are family owned and lack sophistication. Since they are private, there is insufficient tracking or data. The result is that financing for Canadian business is more difficult.

According to Leon, "financing coincides with two broad timeframes: when a business is in trouble or when a business is growing. In either case, our task is to locate the financing and structure a deal." To successfully achieve this, he developed a system based on lessons learned from his past positions. Like many professionals committed to private equity, the source of his experience is based on a stint in public markets. I am impressed by how often knowledge of public equity has been adapted to private equity.

His previous success involved 'market intelligence'; i.e. the knowledge of what clients were buying and selling and he became masterful at utilizing market information. 'Market intelligence' is the basis of his firm, ZED Financial, and what makes it unique.

In 2002, after the dotcom bubble burst, there was a shortage of capital and private businesses were struggling to obtain financing. Leon and his partner decided to build a boutique investment bank focused on private equity where they could efficiently unite a business in search of funding with an appropriate PE firm or debt provider. "We flew to New York and Chicago, and spent time learning about American private equity and how firms differentiated themselves. Within the United States, both cities are known as 'money centers'; that is, they are hubs where much financing originates."

"We wanted to understand the knowledge or 'market intelligence' gathered in these centers. In order to finance Canadian businesses, we wanted to know where the money was, what the various PE firms were buying, in what locations, their typical deal size, and which financing vehicles (debt or equity) they favoured. In the U.S., PE firms are highly specialized, we knew that each firm is best at something and wanted to understand their respective strengths. Our goal was to catalogue this information in order to help finance Canadian businesses."

They invested thousands of hours building relationships which resulted in a database that allows them to access the best choices for each business in need of capital. The database requires on-going updates and ZED employs two people to maintain and keep the database current. Their database contains 600-700 PE firms and 300 debt providers. ZED is like a matchmaking service. Although there are similar database businesses in the U.S. that sell comparable information, their database is proprietary and used for their own purposes.

"When a business owner comes to me, I look at the financials and know if a deal will fly. I can weed out unsuitable deals quickly." Leon says. "Once the financials seem hopeful, we search the database for the 15-20 PE firms that match the parameters of the business in search of capital."

The parties to a potential deal should share at least three characteristics. For example, the PE firm advancing money has previous experience in the same industry, has worked with businesses in a similar region and provides the right type of financing, be it debt or equity.

I asked why businesses can't do this type of legwork themselves and find their own financing partners.

"Many PE firms that claim an interest in financing are generalists who have never done a similar deal and are learning the industry as they go. Therefore, the financing is dragged out and in danger of not closing. This is devastating for the business that is counting on the capital. In contrast, a PE firm that has been involved in similar deals has a feel for the situation and tends to make quicker and better decisions. Business owners receive better terms from lenders or purchasers with experience in their industry."

I remembered an insight from a different interview, "In private equity, a quick 'no' is better than a slow 'yes'."

Leon then listed the three main reasons that businesses fail to land their financing. He calls these 'blown up deals':

"The first reason that deals blow up is a *deal killer issue*. For example, the designated PE firm spends months investigating and while doing due diligence finds there is an environmental problem where it has no experience and so walks away."

"The second reason for financing failure is *deal fatigue*: a PE firm inexperienced in a particular industry drags out the process, goes overboard on their due diligence, thus frustrating the business owners and hindering the owner's progress."

"The final reason is *bait and switch*. This does not necessarily occur because a PE firm is out to mislead, but the partners may not necessarily understand the business and so they find last-minute issues. The PE firm tries to re-price the financing and meanwhile the business has become desperate for money, resulting in disappointing terms."

ZED's database helps to circumvent these situations by prequalifying the buyers. Once they have identified the potential PE firm or debt provider, they prepare a proposal tailored to the buyer's specifications.

Unless the database can locate 15-20 candidates that have the knowledge and the right parameters for a particular financing, ZED will not proceed. This large number is necessary because of the high failure rate: one-third of the financing candidates drop out immediately (perhaps they are fully committed) and one-third are too slow to react, leaving only the remaining third to indicate some interest. This small remaining group continues to shrink until a match is found.

Leon told me about a deal of which he is particularly proud. "A biotech firm approached us. Not only was this firm pre-profit but there was pending litigation against it. It seemed like a long shot but our database revealed several PE firms interested in the biotech area. A financing match was made and the buyer completed its due diligence in a record three weeks." The moral of this story is that the terms and conditions offered by a financier are based on its perception of risk. Where a financier has previous experience in similar situations the price offered to the business is more appropriate. There is less work and a greater chance of closing.

Leon maintains that ZED often works with difficult deals or dislocated industries. He claims if a business in his size range is financeable, he is the most likely to succeed because of his database. He feels the firm excels in finding the right partner.

Leon is adamant about the potential harm to a business with the wrong financing. "If a business selects the wrong capital provider, it could struggle with an unreliable partner who could damage its capital structure and make it difficult to obtain future financing. Clients need to live with whoever is doing their financing."

I asked Leon why a business owner wouldn't go directly to an M&A firm which both provides advice and helps in finding financial partners. He claimed that M&A firms use an imprecise approach that is too broad in its sweep. He compared ZED to a rifle; quick and targeted. I would imagine that ZED is most suitable for owners who know exactly what they are looking for and do not have the time or feel the need for advice.

SHOTGUNS: A MAVERICK APPROACH

Conversation with Jim Ambrose,
Partner, The Shotgun Fund

I was on the look out for a few PE firms that cater to small businesses. These businesses are more representative of the Canadian market and often struggle to find equity financing. One firm caught my attention: The Shotgun Fund. Unlike most PE firms which are generalists, The Shotgun Fund has found a niche, concentrates on difficult to find financing for small businesses ($5 million to $15 million in enterprise value) and has a rapid turnaround. It can often complete a deal in 30 days.

A 'shotgun' provision is part of a standard agreement when people go into business together. Its aim is to protect the partners if there is a falling out. The provision allows one partner to notify the others of his intention to purchase their shares, usually on short notice. The other partners must accept the offer or else turn around and agree to buy out the triggering partner on the same basis.

This clause is included with good intent; it allows either partner to back out of an unsatisfactory partnership. The problem is that it can be used against weaker partners at a particularly vulnerable time. To add to the distress, shotguns are usually fired on a Friday before a long holiday, such as between Christmas and New Year's, when it is difficult to muster the proper resources.

In 1999, an owner of a successful Ontario firm appeared at the office of Jim Ambrose, an investment professional who invested in small businesses. The owner was distraught because his partner had triggered a 'shotgun' at a low price. The adversarial partner knew the limited financial resources of his partner and saw a chance to acquire the business cheaply. Jim Ambrose's firm stepped in with funding. Ambrose's firm saw an opportunity and immediately registered the name: 'The Shotgun Fund'.

At that time, private equity was not a buzz word. The hot tickets were technology and venture capital. Registering the name 'The Shotgun Fund' was fresh thinking. A professional (C.A. or lawyer), who typed the word 'shotgun' into his browser or saw the ads, knew instantly what it meant.

"One of our most successful deals," brags Jim, "came around Christmas from a lawyer with a devastated client who was rejected by the bank. The client was on the verge of losing his business amidst the festivities. A Canadian lawyer did an Internet search and found the 'Shotgun Fund'. Our firm was accessed and the deal was completed at the 11th hour. It was one of The Shotgun Fund's largest and fastest deals, completed in only four days."

Back then, this also seemed like an edgy/controversial business, because shotguns can be pulled when there is a dispute and generally at the most injurious time: over vacations, when there are medical problems or during divorce proceedings. Often shotguns are a sign of human greed, the more aggressive partner wants the whole business for himself and finds an opportunity to take advantage of a situation. Jim Ambrose feels that his fund helps even the score and do deals that protect the weaker party. The victim keeps his share and The Shotgun Fund generally replaces the departing shareholder.

The niche created by The Shotgun Fund gives it access to profitable businesses. What the firm likes about shotgun deals is that three things are known; that a transaction must happen, the price, and the closing date. In addition to shotguns, the firm focuses on any deal that requires prompt action. For example, a competitor goes into bankruptcy and a strategic buyer needs money immediately to buy the assets.

Jim claims that The Shotgun Fund can do the due diligence, check references and come to a prompt decision. "The reason for the quick turnaround is that we deal directly with the principals, not agents or institutions. The Shotgun Fund's clients didn't inherit their business; they built the business and can continue running it after separating from a partner." The direct nature of the model is The Shotgun Fund's attraction, but it must be nimble. It does not get involved in competitions, or auctions. Conversely, most private equity financiers do not take an interest in The Shotgun Fund type deals.

I am curious to know if these shotguns, that are a result of an adversarial relationship, tend to be generally problematic. In other words, is there a higher failure rate to the deals done by The Shotgun Fund?

Jim says that is not the case, but they do make judgment calls about the individuals. "We study the motivation for pulling the shotgun. A person who pulls a shotgun may not be good partner material and may have a history of blowing away partners. Sometimes, the person firing the shotgun is not running the business on a day-to-day basis." This is the case when a shotgun is fired by a financial partner with deep pockets or a competitor with a conflict of interest. "Our firm must feel confident that there is a legitimate dispute and that we are backing the right party".

The firm has strict parameters for the businesses it backs. They must be profitable, have been in business for three years, be of a certain size (at least $20 million in sales) and be reasonably priced. To protect itself, The Shotgun Fund charges its due diligence and legal fees to the party seeking financing. This covers some of the fund's costs if the deal falls through.

I press Jim on problems that The Shotgun Fund faces in such partnerships.

"Compensation can be a bone of contention." Jim says, "The founding partners often cleaned out the till at the end of the year, whereas with The Shotgun Fund the remaining partner is paid an annual income until the business is sold. The salary is negotiated, but as time goes by the partner who is left may try to claim more."

"Mainly, the original partners frustrated each other, because they managed jointly, often on a daily basis. In the case of The Shotgun Fund, the only fights over business decisions are board fights." This is because The Shotgun Fund takes its ownership position seriously. It insists on equal representation on the board and an equal vote on important issues. Although its goal is to provide replacement capital so one party can keep the business and run with it, decisions must also be in the best interests of The Shotgun Fund.

"Initially when The Shotgun Fund steps in, the partner who stays can be mistrustful; with time he appreciates our professional experience and resources" Jim maintains.

Giving up equity is not a cheap form of financing. Sometimes the remaining partner might have been better off hunting for debt financing. Certainly, in the long run, if the business succeeds, debt would have been cheaper. However, many operating partners don't like debt, because if they hit a short-term snag, the debt could put them under.

Jim ends by saying that The Shotgun Fund focuses on small, interesting deals in a niche market and his firm survives by sticking to its model. "One of our biggest frustrations is waiting for suitable transactions. Often we wait a long time for the right deal."

As I found my way around the private equity community, Jim's name came up a few times as a maverick. Niches or specialties, such as The Shotgun Fund, are a good sign, because they make the private equity industry efficient and more competitive. Particularly in Canada where PE firms tend to be both generalists and homogeneous, it is noteworthy to see firms that differentiate themselves.

FINDING THE BEST PE FUNDS

Conversation with Thomas R. Kennedy,
Partner, Kensington Capital Partners Limited

It was a glorious Friday afternoon in June; the city was empty as people headed off early for a weekend at the cottage. My husband and I were betting that my 3:00 p.m. interview on such a day would be cancelled. Perhaps we were hoping for this outcome so we could join the fleeing throngs. We were wrong and the interview proceeded as scheduled. It spoke volumes of a man's dedication to his work. I gathered from several such encounters that long, demanding hours were a consistent feature of private equity.

The purpose of this interview was to examine private equity from the investor's perspective. I turned to Kensington Capital Partners, which runs an FOF (Fund of Funds), and met with one of its partners, Thomas Kennedy. FOFs invest in several PE funds and hence diversify across investment styles, industries, business sizes and geographic regions. Since an FOF creates private equity portfolios by investing in the PE funds of others, they should be expert at finding the best PE firms.

Tom outlined the purpose of investing in private equity. "The goal in private equity is to earn twice as much as you can in public markets over a five to ten year period. Otherwise, based on its shortcomings, lack of liquidity and limited regulation, private equity investing is not worth the effort." If private equity managers try to mimic an index as is the practice in public markets, their performance is mediocre and becomes similar to average returns in public markets. Why subject yourself to mediocre returns if you can't improve on your upside?

In Tom's words, "private equity must produce 10% more per year than a reasonable expectation for public markets. In private equity you must earn two or three times your capital every five years to make the investment worthwhile."

Tom then explained how this need for sizable returns impacts the functioning of PE firms. "The U.S. has a very healthy and mature private equity market with 1000s of PE firms. The majority struggle, produce mediocre returns and eventually fall off the map. Private equity has reached a stage where you can't raise money and stay in business unless you show superior performance."

Based on our discussion in early 2008, the spread between a mediocre PE firm and the top ones had widened to the point where PE firms wouldn't survive without high returns exceeding 18%-20% annually. On the other hand, at 30%, firms could easily raise money, so that became the expectation. He even alluded to outstanding returns of 50% per year among top PE funds.

His bottom line, "Stick with the top quartile of PE firms that offer the best returns in order to justify the risk."

"To achieve high returns, you need people with operating experience who can walk in the owners' shoes," Tom claimed. "The best private equity managers must dig in, reinforce business management, and grow the business. How are they going to do this if they have never run a business, don't know how to motivate personnel, meet a payroll, deal with unions or build and shut down factories?"

When a PE firm buys a business, the best firms know what they are looking for before they close the deal. They can put all the elements together in a matter of months to effect change. For example, their plans can include new products, entering new markets or the development of an innovative new strategy.

"Top teams are off and running before the deal is signed," he said. Execution on their plan is accomplished three to five months after closing and the PE firm doesn't flinch. It is the private equity group's unique experience that is brought to bear to enhance value; they know where they are going and work closely with business management to achieve their ends.

In order to devise a workable plan, these teams are well versed in a narrow base of industries and bring with them a deep and broad network of contacts. They know the appropriate bankers and competitors. This allows them to research and create a credible action plan. However, before team members can raise the capital to run a PE fund, they must prove they can generate strong returns. This makes the barriers to entry high.

Some professionals try to create a track record by investing their own capital in a preliminary fund before they attempt to market a fund or attract outside capital. Others build a reputation, working for sponsoring organizations like banks or insurance companies. It is only after the principals have achieved outstanding performance that they have the credibility to raise capital for a fund. If their first fund fails, second chances are hard to come by.

"The problem for investors is accessing the best private equity managers, because the top PE firms are not widely known. Finding the best PE firms and monitoring them is difficult. The disadvantage of private equity is that investors lack the help they would receive in public markets. Investors don't have the benefit of research staff employed by investment dealers in public equities, who identify, analyze, and track opportunities."

Tom offered some basic suggestions for selecting PE firms and recommends that investors develop their own rigorous process. Private equity offers a chance for institutions and individuals who enjoy doing investigative work to develop a selection process.

When I worked as an investment advisor, I was often amazed at the flimsy basis on which investment decisions in private equity were made. Often investments were concluded based on word of mouth from a family member, friend or colleague. Here are some more solid criteria suggested by Tom:

Investigate the people managing the PE firm. The best PE firms are well established. Creating a list of open-ended questions, and talking with knowledgeable associates of the firm, is probably the best way to kick the tires. Ask to meet a cross section of people the firm has dealt with; business owners, executives employed in their portfolio businesses, investors in previous funds, lawyers, accountants and bankers. Find out about outsiders' experience doing business with a particular PE firm.

Tom recommends, "Talk to board members: Did the PE firm work with management? Did they show up for board meetings? Did they participate and seem knowledgeable about the affairs of the business? Were they cooperative with management?"

Study the track record. In private equity, making money should be more consistent than in public markets. Public markets are more affected by external matters and market psychology. Good public managers, using styles such as value or growth, can be in or out of phase at various times. In private equity, managers work with businesses and are instrumental in their growth over a period of years. Therefore, the true value added by a PE firm is not as influenced by external matters.

Tom adds, "Confirm the track record. Don't take the fund's word as gospel. How did they calculate the track record? Did they leave out businesses in which they lost money?"

Know the funds' bench strength. What are characteristics that have led to the PE firms' past success? Who works there and how are they remunerated? Is the current firm populated by the same people?

Since Tom is adamant that PE firms include professionals with operating experience, he includes his own rule of thumb for judging the GP. He asks, "If key business executives suddenly left, does the GP have the people to step in and take immediate charge?" The scorecard for any PE fund is how well it can grow its businesses over the next five years. So, invest in funds where the GP has in-depth expertise in the businesses.

Watch out for style drift. Make sure that PE firms are following the same patterns they have in the past. If a PE firm has succeeded based on its unique method, it must now duplicate the same process. You are buying their history.

Access to information. Paradoxically, information on private businesses is more available to its investors than in public markets. Public businesses are more secretive, because in public markets every investor must have the same information at the same time. Public management must be consistent in the release of information and there are regulators to enforce this. In private markets, the flow of information is more accessible and good PE firms send investors whatever they need. PE firms must be willing to share that information with investors in its fund.

Competitive information is treated the same in both public and private markets. For example, neither public nor private businesses will disclose the purchase or sale of a business until the transaction is completed. Overall, the flow of information for private portfolio businesses is outstanding and there is no reason for a lack of transparency to its investors.

After a thorough investigation of a PE firm, Tom concluded that investors are equipped to ask themselves the following questions: "What is it about the PE firm's experience that makes me believe I can trust them?" and "How will the fund manager reduce risk and enhance success?"

I confronted Tom with a nagging doubt. I am concerned that we have discussed the past at length, but as every public prospectus will warn: past performance is no guarantee of the future. How can investors protect themselves against poor performance in the future? There was a pause as Tom goes on to talk about contractual protection.

"Make sure you can fire the GP," Tom says, "It should be in the documentation and it should be practical and not theoretical. You want a low threshold to vote out the GP. If enough people feel they don't like the GP, the LPs should be able to get rid of him without unnecessary hoops."

"Of course, make sure your interests are aligned with the GPs," Tom continued. "You lose, they lose. They must have a substantial interest in a fund on the same terms and conditions you do."

"How do you figure that out?" I asked.

"Ask," he says, "You are investing and have a right to know. Ask how much they are putting in and what percentage this represents of their net worth. At the same time make sure the individuals are at risk and that they have not transferred the risk to a company with no assets."

Tom ends by pointing out that an FOF can take up to six months on this type of due diligence before it makes a commitment to picking a PE fund. This is because a good FOF manager pools the capital of several investors and therefore has the resources to research the best PE funds. Meanwhile, an investor who decides to invest through an FOF can use similar criteria to select the best FOF.

On its website, Kensington points out the significant risks within private equity and claims that the reason to invest with an FOF is to reduce this risk. They argue that the probability of total loss in a single private equity investment is greater than 30%. The probability of some loss by investing in a PE fund is also over 30% and thus remains high. However, by investing through an FOF "the probability of any loss being realized by an investor has been shown to be almost entirely eliminated."[19] (It will be interesting to see if this statement holds up through the meltdown.) Kensington concludes that the negligible levels of loss justify the additional fees paid to an FOF manager.

Before I left, Tom expressed his optimism for the future of private equity. "Ten years ago there were few ways an investor could participate in Canadian private equity; now there are numerous possibilities." Private equity is a growing discipline. Going forward, he feels, there is greater scope for the private equity industry to expand than is the case for public equity. Despite its recent expansion, the private equity industry is still very small relative to public markets.

---

19. Kensington Capital Website as of 2008, Kensington Capital Partners: Why Fund of Funds.

PART IV
THE CONTROVERSY

THE DARK SIDE OF PRIVATE EQUITY

"The good times masked inefficiencies and covered mistakes. How many of the returns of the last ten years in private equity were a 'sham' driven by aggressive leverage and over-priced businesses as opposed to real value creation?"

Tony Melman, a Founding Partner,
Onex Corporation

When the Berlin Wall fell in 1989, capitalist countries were in a self-congratulatory mood. The fall represented not only a political victory but an economic one as well. The communist economy had imploded and East Berliners who poured into the West wanted economic benefits as well as political freedom. Professionals working in public markets celebrated the triumph of free public markets over controlled communist ones.

At its height in early 2007, professionals in private equity had the same euphoric attitude towards their business model. They believed the private equity model had surpassed that of public equity. There was repeated reference to private equity alignment of interests, more realistic time horizons and efficient business management. For several years, private equity had markedly outperformed public markets, especially in Canada. But in the latter half of 2007, this confidence began to falter as prominent private equity deals turned sour.

Blackstone, an icon American PE firm which went public in 2007, reported an 89% plunge in earnings in the first quarter of 2008. Within a year of their public offerings, crème de la crème American PE firms, such as Blackstone and Fortress Investment Group, watched their stock price drop over 50%. Angry debates ensued, followed by a reassessment of the private equity model. Had PE firms strayed from their original principles? At the end of March of 2008, as earnings plummeted, Blackstone's assets under administration increased 47% from a year earlier.[20]

Had they turned into asset gatherers dependent on management fees instead of being motivated by the 'carry'? By raising ever larger pools of capital and generating greater fee revenue, such firms could be sustained by sizeable fees regardless of poor performance in their portfolio companies. In addition, some PE firms extracted extra fees from their portfolio companies. For example, they charged the portfolio company 4% to buy it on top of the 2% management fee.

During 2008, as the recession deepened, increasing numbers of bankruptcies among private equity portfolio companies raised suspicion even further. Most bankruptcies occurred in companies overburdened with debt. Originally, the meltdown exposed the poorly managed financial sector and the limits of unregulated free markets. There was disappointment and disbelief over the lack of oversight, transparency and accountability. Fear spread as financial institutions failed and investment values plunged. The result was global and system-wide panic. Excesses in private equity were also exposed, bloated with debt, its image was equally tarnished.

Alan Greenspan, once popular Chairman of the Federal Reserve, admitted that his belief in the ability of financial institutions to act in their own best interests without regulation was a mistake. Working in government, perhaps he did not comprehend the pressure on bankers to compete and show regular quarterly earnings growth. Similar problems surrounded private equity where bankers earned a great deal from transaction fees and ancillary services. Bankers hungry for the next private equity deal had mispriced risk. They let down their guard and lent too aggressively.

The landscape has changed as a result of the meltdown. Financial institutions will not be trusted without better regulation. When financial institutions fail, they jeopardize everyone's financial wellbeing and society pays the price. The meltdown will change the way private equity operates as the excessive leverage that fueled it will be harder to come by.

Debt and More Debt

A key element in buyouts is debt. Prior to the meltdown, loans were cheap and plentiful while rising market values kept credit flowing. Some PE

---

20.   Roddy Boyd, "Private Equity Shops Feel Blackstone's Pain", *Fortune*, March 10, 2008.

firms recklessly took advantage of this environment, loading their businesses with huge debts backed by minimal equity. Conversely, because credit was so accessible, the price of businesses kept rising. In the meltdown, the most significant victims are large buyouts with highly-leveraged financing structures.

Typically, PE firms leveraged their buyouts with one-quarter equity and three-quarters debt, but as time went on the equity layers became even thinner. In the aborted BCE deal, which would have been the largest leveraged buyout in history, the proposed equity was $8 billion and the required borrowing was over $43 billion out of a $51.7 billion deal. Equity would have represented only 16% of the total with debt at 84%. Many argued this was too much debt for a mismanaged company in need of restructuring. Ultimately, the BCE deal fell through because of changing times. However, many buyouts were completed with such thin margins of equity that they were compared to the subprime debacle. Too much lent with too little down. It gets worse...

Even riskier were the cash flow ratios (debt/cash flow); the higher the ratio the higher the risk, because cash flow is required to cover interest and to pay down debt. Low ratios mean there is a good cushion of cash being generated to pay the debt. If the operating profits should fall, you would still have a healthy margin of safety. Think of paying your mortgage after taking a salary cut. If the mortgage is small compared to your reduced salary, you may still get by.

In the early days of private equity, debt was no more than five times EBITDA (earnings before interest, taxation, depreciation and amortization). During the final years of the credit boom, the debt rose as high as nine and ten times EBITDA. At these levels, even a small drop in profits endangers the ability of a business to pay the debt. In addition, deteriorating lending standards added to the problems...

Not only did PE firms contribute too little equity and resort to risky ratios of debt to cash flow, but the safeguards used by lenders to monitor debt repayment were also removed. Ordinarily, when PE firms borrow money for a business purchase, conditions are imposed that give lenders influence over borrowers. A borrower has to comply with these conditions (or covenants) in order to maintain the loan. If the borrower is in breach, the lender can demand repayment of the loan. This permits the lender to monitor the loan: the borrower is required on a quarterly basis to meet financial tests, such as the ratio of debt to cash flow.

These safeguards provide an early warning system for lenders: if a business does not pass its tests, the bank can demand repayment or renegotiate the loan. Unfortunately, prior to the meltdown many loans were issued with few or no maintenance tests. These diminished standards were referred to as 'covenant-lite'. 'Covenant-lite' loans suggest a loosening of credit conditions which remove important safeguards needed by lenders to protect their capital from a faltering business. As with the sub-prime debacle, 'covenant-lite' loans posed questions about risks to the wider economy...

Another lending policy that would make ordinary business people cringe involves 'bullet debt'. This is non-amortized debt, where no capital repayments are required for a pre-agreed period, often around eight years, after which large payments fall due. The benefit to the borrower is that it allows a business to preserve short-term cash flow for business growth. The risk is to the lender because private equity debt usually includes several layers of subordinate debt below the senior level. If debt has few protective covenants, the lender of subordinate debt is left holding the bag in a business failure because there are no assets left at the end to repay the subordinate loan.[21]

Many PE firms risked too little of their own equity and limited their losses through heavy borrowing. This led to irresponsible risk-taking. In a recession, businesses saddled with too much debt become incapable of supporting the loans. The issues surrounding private equity have deepened since the meltdown and they involve systemic failures. As a result, there is concern that large business failures will reverberate through the economy and further undermine our financial system. To avoid such impact, experts feel that there will need to be more cautious use of private equity leverage in the future. This might occur automatically if interest rates rise, making future deals less profitable.

Private Contractual Agreements

The 'private' in private equity now raises doubts about undisclosed financial problems. The need for transparency in large private business transactions is becoming an on-going theme and there are calls for greater regulation. To understand the regulatory issues surrounding private equity, it is necessary to return to its roots.

When PE firms began in the 1970s, they focused on small to mid-sized business deals. Capital was directed towards venture or growth opportunities. Venture capital involved taking small ownership stakes at an early stage of business development. Alternatively, growth capital involved business funding

---

21. Veral V. Acharya, Julian Franks and Henri Servaes, *Private Equity: Boom and Bust?*, London Business School, CEPR, and ECGI, U.K., Fall, 2007.

at a critical stage of expansion where investors, in exchange for their cash, took a minority stake in a business. Since the scope of PE firms was limited and their financial repercussions minor, rules and regulations were determined by private contracts on an ad hoc basis.[22]

PE firms and LPs (often pension funds) decided on the terms for entering into an agreement. Regulation and reporting were governed by the contractual relationship between GPs and LPs and were put in place at the time of the LPs' commitment. Often deals of that size and nature did not involve a change of ownership and so did not require transparency, public regulation or any unique oversight.

Small and mid-sized deals are still the mainstay of private equity, particularly in Canada. However, the private equity industry has evolved to the point where buyout activity is now the largest part of the industry. By definition, buyouts involve a change of control or new ownership, both of which carry significant risks. Although by the number of transactions, smaller and medium sized deals are the majority, large buyouts can cause seismic repercussions socially and economically. Buyouts affect more than just the shareholders; they affect employees, suppliers, customers, their environment and the community. These other groups, impacted by buyouts, are called stakeholders.

The impact of some large buyouts has raised red flags about the contractual nature of private equity. There must be a better understanding of how private equity works and its contribution to the overall economy. Should private equity be subject to more scrutiny, better public accountability and social legitimacy?[23]

Buyouts can create great anxiety for employees and can have a negative impact on employment and working conditions. They might pose a threat to the short-term stability of a business and its long-term sustainability. Going forward, rising interest rates could lead to a cascading collapse of leveraged buyouts and other businesses dependent on them.

There is concern that the secretiveness and insensitivity of private contractual agreements hurt non-owner stakeholders. As private equity reaches

---

22. For further details, see *Guidelines for Disclosure and Transparency in Private Equity*, report by Sir David Walker, for the BVCA (British Venture Capital Association) and a group of major private equity firms, November 20, 2007.

23. For further details, see *Guidelines for Disclosure and Transparency in Private Equity*, report by Sir David Walker, for the BVCA (British Venture Capital Association) and a group of major private equity firms, November 20, 2007.

maturity in the next phase of its growth, we could create a healthier, stronger industry with more openness, input and public awareness. Should private equity always be private? Increasing dialogue and greater awareness addresses the impact of private equity on societal issues and the economy at large.

Perhaps it is time to redefine private equity by deal size for the purpose of new guidelines. In large private equity deals, there could be more public account-ability and the obligation to communicate in a timely and effective manner with all stakeholders. Those buyouts having a large impact on a region could formal-ize their relationship with stakeholders. This makes it easier to plan around issues that involve local employment, environmental and community issues.

At this time, there are two extremes in reporting requirements: disclosure for public companies is very strict, whereas the same business in private hands has few disclosure requirements with little monitoring. At worst, the behaviour of buyouts has been described as 'buy it, strip it, and flip it'.

Socially responsible investing is a major tenant for many individuals and institutions. As an advisor, I worked with individual investors who ada-mantly refused to invest in an industry regardless of its profitability if the social consequences were harmful (e.g. tobacco companies). Institutions, charities and endowments, because of their reputational risk, are also sensi-tive to social issues.

I believe that what is best for society is ultimately also best for investors. Therefore, I advocate some disclosure guidelines and transparency for a health-ier private equity industry. Currently, Canadian private equity is governed solely by private contractual agreements.

Investor Protection

Most of the investors in buyouts are government or quasi-governmental institutions. Institutional investors such as public sector pension plans account for over half of the total investment in private equity buyouts either through direct investing or PE funds. The other half is controlled by sovereign wealth funds (SWF), endowments or wealthy individuals. Sovereign wealth funds rep-resent state investments that are generally funded from their foreign currency reserves. They are pools of capital that foreign governments, such as China, Norway, Singapore, Abu Dhabi, etc. invest on behalf of their citizens.

There was initially little demand for private equity oversight to protect its investors because so many investors were members of large sophisticated institutions. Smaller investors had limited access to PE funds, so there was no serious call for transparency, better reporting or ensuring investor protection.

The result is a vicious circle, as the lack of transparency and regulation inhibits future investors. This is borne out by a study in Canada showing public sector pension plans and $5 billion-plus-Canadian institutions are the most active private equity investors. In contrast to the U.S., smaller Canadian institutions, such as endowments, foundations and corporate pensions are reluctant to participate.[24]

One reason cited by smaller institutions for not embracing Canadian private equity is skepticism about performance data. Smaller Canadian institutions are frustrated by how PE funds value their portfolio assets. PE funds are long-term investments, often a decade long, so that valuations are important for interim performance results. Before the wind-up of a fund, how do you determine your performance if there is no clarity and transparency in the valuation method?[25]

When there are no universally accepted standards for valuing assets or for performance measurement, how can investors shop and compare PE funds? PE firms are not obliged to adhere to standards for performance presentation and there is in fact no consistency. Therefore, a quality firm that is fundraising can't compete against less reputable peers with aggressive metrics. Until investors can compare apples to apples and performance numbers are put in a standardized format, high returns in private equity will not be perceived as legitimate. At a minimum for investors, there must be the reassurance of standardized accounting and reporting guidelines in order to compare the track records of different PE funds.

In Canada, there are no standardized accounting or reporting requirements, no rules for the timing or frequency of reports, no compliance procedures or governing bodies with oversight and monitoring authority. This is in sharp contrast to public equity markets.

To foster the growth of the private equity industry and investor confidence, three areas require more transparency:

24. SME Financing Data Initiative – *Finding the Key: Canadian Institutional Investors and Private Equity*, Government of Canada, September 15, 2008.

25. For further details, see *Finding the Key: Canadian Institutional Investors and Private Equity*, Project Conducted by Macdonald & Associates Limited, June, 2004, SME Financing Data Initiative, Government of Canada, Information Distribution Centre, Communications and Marketing Branch, Industry Canada.

(i)   Analysis and assessment of the industry as a whole,

(ii)   Reporting standards for individual PE firms

(iii)   Enhanced reporting by the businesses they own.[26]

The private equity industry is now sufficiently large that benchmarking of it alongside public equity is required. Investors need evidence that private equity genuinely adds value commensurate with its risk and illiquidity. There is a need for authoritative analysis that confirms private equity's contribution to the growth of earnings and enterprise value in businesses. Studies can be done that separate performance due to leverage and financial structuring from true business growth. Without confirmation, naysayers argue that private equity is overleveraging business, that the holding period for the average private equity business is too short and that businesses are sucked dry particularly in the last few years of a PE fund. This does not inspire investor confidence.

PE firms are not credible if there are no best practices or reasonable expectations for them. If there are no standards to support the industry, there will be no investment advisors to assess PE firms and no analyst recommendations. There must be a market infrastructure to tempt investors and reassure them regarding the viability of their investments.

In the ideal world private equity may well be a better model, as its practitioners believe, but in the real world ideals are not always upheld. If investors examine the history of private equity in Canada, there was a dark period in the late 1980s and early 1990s, when private equity underperformed and institutional investors abandoned it. This period was marked by severe disputes with GPs. The most serious ones pertained to misalignment of the GPs interests. Alignment of interests has been emphasized throughout this book as a major tenant of private equity, but in practice there is no set standard.

Practitioners fearing the consequences of the meltdown argue that PE firms should publish more information for their investors and timely updates on their structure and investment approach. For example, conflicts of interest should be more clearly disclosed. There are even concerns regarding the remuneration for different partners at PE firms.

Europe and the U.K. have been leaders in urging better industry standards and best practices. In Canada, the industry association CVCA (Canada's

---

26.   For further details, see *Guidelines for Disclosure and Transparency in Private Equity*, report by Sir David Walker, for the BVCA (British Venture Capital Association) and a group of major private equity firms, November 20, 2007.

Venture Capital and Private Equity Association), recently acknowledged the importance of establishing industry standards within the context of more consistent and precise global standards.

Best practices, regulation and compliance are signs of a mature market. This infrastructure will come in one of two ways. Governance will evolve as the industry grows or it will be forced upon them by an attention-grabbing failure.

Teaming Up for Advantageous Terms

Because of private equity's unregulated nature, collaborating is not uncommon for large institutions where one investor acts as the lead for an investor syndicate. The community of institutional investors in private equity worldwide is so small that there is a club atmosphere among them making it easy to compare notes.

Unlike a listed public corporation which has an average of 150,000 investors, a typical PE fund contains around 10 to 30 LPs.[27] With so few investors in a fund and since they remain together for a long time, approximately ten years, teaming up is a distinct possibility. There is comfort in knowing the other investors with similar interests.

In the end, private equity is a people business. Financial models and investment parameters provide a limited snapshot of a GP. Due diligence involves knowing more details of who is making key decisions, buying, managing and selling businesses.

When a GP has a good track record, investors tend to subscribe for subsequent PE funds; this is called a 'roll over'. Investors considering a PE fund can ask the GP for a list of other potential investors. This is awkward for the GP, since he must ask permission from these investors, but it is probably the best background check. Investors in previous funds can also be canvassed regarding their experience; why they invested, and if they intend to invest in the latest PE fund. If not, why not?

Similarly, smaller investors have been known to band together, assemble a team and appoint a spokesperson to speak collectively. This is a good way of managing the process of evaluating a PE fund. If approximately half a dozen

---

27. For further details, see *Guidelines for Disclosure and Transparency in Private Equity*, report by Sir David Walker, for the BVCA (British Venture Capital Association) and a group of major private equity firms, November 20, 2007.

investors are assembled to act as a syndicate, they can use the same law firm to represent them.

A syndicate, using the same law firm, has leverage over the GP and can negotiate terms. There are many details in a PE fund that are subject to negotiation, such as fees, provisions for getting rid of a GP who is not doing a good job, and claw-back of previous profits from a GP after a loss. A successful PE firm may not agree to these terms. Nevertheless, investors who are not prepared to perform extensive due diligence and are inadequately represented are better off avoiding this asset class until there are better standards and more regulation.

The years after the meltdown represent an opportunity for private equity investors. Pension plans have a unique advantage, because of ongoing premiums paid by plan members; they have the opportunity to buy reasonably priced businesses and enhance their long-term returns. In the post-meltdown environment, cash is king and any investor with cash resources will have a rare investment opportunity. Because Canada is at an early stage of private equity, hopefully we will show leadership in lifting the veil of secrecy and lead the way towards better industry standards.

BCE: THE WORLD'S ALMOST BIGGEST LEVERAGED BUYOUT[28]

The attempted BCE deal will go down as an historic event and no book on Canadian private equity would be complete without a discussion of its significance. Once a powerhouse of the Canadian stock market, BCE, Canada's largest telecom company, deteriorated at a time when its industry was becoming one of the market's hottest growth sectors. Its decisions present a perfect study of the shortcomings of the public equity model. How could a leading company at the right place at the right time go so wrong?

In the end, after years of decline, BCE became a takeover target by private equity interests. The takeover, at almost $52 billion, would have represented the biggest private acquisition in Canadian history and the world's largest leveraged buyout ever. Since there is a pending $1.2 billion lawsuit against the bidders, Teachers' and its partners, the parties themselves are barred from telling their story.

BCE used to be my largest client holding, not because I always recommended the stock as an investment advisor, but because Canadian families inherited it. Founded in 1880 as the Bell Telephone Company of Canada Ltd., BCE was one of Canada's most widely held stocks. Certainly in Ontario, owning BCE was tantamount to a family tradition and selling it was taboo. It was considered a 'widows and orphans' stock because of its low risk and steady dividend. In 1968, the company was renamed Bell Canada. When I started in 1975, Bell Canada was listed as the fifth largest company in the country and one of its most prized and important establishments.

Bad Buys

Between 1980 and 1997, the federal government gradually deregulated the telecom industry and Bell Canada's monopoly ended. Part of Bell's response to this policy was to form a holding company called Bell Canada Enterprises (BCE) in 1983. BCE would hold Bell Canada but it could also diversify into a variety of businesses and become a conglomerate. This strategy proved to be the utility's undoing.

When BCE purchased Montreal Trustco in March of 1989, I wondered what the two had in common. Montreal Trustco was a provider of diversified financial and trust services whereas BCE was Canada's largest telecoms com-

---

28. No one at either BCE or Teachers' was available for comment concerning BCE because of pending litigation. Hence, this information was gathered from public sources.

pany. The only thing they had in common was age. Montreal Trustco was a 100-year-old company, founded in 1889.

Sure enough, the acquisition was unsuccessful and in December, 1993 Montreal Trustco along with Brookfield Development Corporation (a real estate company), both in totally unrelated businesses to BCE, were sold for a special after-tax charge (write-off). Montreal Trustco, purchased for $875 million was sold for $400 million, less than half its original purchase price.

BCE's ill-conceived diversification continued when it acquired control of Teleglobe, an overseas telecom company, in 2000. Under the direction of Jean Monty who was both CEO and Chairman of the Board, BCE paid $7.4 billion at the height of the high-tech boom to acquire the remaining 77% of Teleglobe it did not already own. Only two years later, in 2002 Teleglobe was under bankruptcy protection. Jean Monty resigned in disgrace.

Teleglobe will go down as the worst Canadian telecoms deal in history, and one of the worst globally. BCE took a massive write off of $7.5 billion to eliminate its holding. BCE had failed to recognize the changing dynamics of Teleglobe's business. During the two years, rates for Teleglobe's data and long distance telephone calls plummeted. Teleglobe's business model had been flawed but where were BCE's watchdogs? Where were the board members who might have safeguarded shareholders against such a fiasco? Why didn't more heads roll?

There was one positive outcome; the positions of chairman of the board and CEO were split as had long been advocated by pension fund investors. Supposedly this would mean more active governance on the part of BCE's board in the future. Richard Currie, previously a supermarket president (Loblaws), was appointed chairman. Michael Sabia, previously a career government bureaucrat, assumed the position of CEO. At a time of massive telecoms change neither had a communications industry background.

Changing Times

The telecommunications industry was humming. Worldwide sales of cell phones, laptops and Blackberries were on a roll. Rogers and Telus had the foresight to expand their wireless divisions. Telus Corp bought Clearnet Communications in 2001. Rogers Communications Inc., once a minor BCE rival, bought Microcell Telecommunications, owner of the Fido brand, in September, 2004.

At that time, Canada offered some of the best worldwide growth prospects for wireless because of low penetration levels; Bell's closest rivals, Rogers and Telus, had the prescience to gobble up everything in sight. In contrast to BCE, Telus appointed a 36-year old, Darren Entwistle, as president and CEO in 2000, a young veteran of the communications industry who made all the right moves. Rogers too, even with an ageing Ted Rogers still in charge, went out on a limb and deeper into debt with its wireless commitment.

Meanwhile, BCE's near-monopoly land line business was in decline and the company lost its early leadership in wireless. By 2006, Bell was earning 18% less revenue per customer and had sharply lower wireless operating profit than its nearest rival, Telus. Around the same time, BCE's CEO, Michael Sabia, took a 455% pay increase.

After BCE sold Telesat in 2006, it was suggested that some of the money be returned to shareholders as compensation for the lethargic stock price. However BCE's chief executive, Michael Sabia, did not approve. A close source commented: "Michael was old-fashioned and he didn't think it was progressive to give shareholders back their own money."[29]

Finally, in a 2007 update to clients, BCE admitted that its balance sheet had been compromised and that its diversification strategy had failed. By this time, shareholders had not seen a dividend increase for 10 years. BCE had failed to prepare the company for a new age. Its stock no longer seemed a good fit for widows and orphans and a remedy was badly needed. One possibility was a merger with Telus. This option had a romantic tone since it would create an 'all-Canadian' telecoms giant. The only potential obstacle was the regulatory concern about competition.

Mysteriously, Telus dropped out of the running just before the deadline for submitting offers to BCE in June of 2007, claiming, "The inadequacies of BCE's bid process did not make it possible for Telus to submit an offer." Other large suitors similarly expressed frustration with BCE's negotiation process and lack of cooperation.

The 'headwinds' of change had confounded BCE. Despite its valuable assets, it was trapped in a mindset where higher rates of return came from asking the regulator for rate increases, where foresight and cooperation were not a

---

29. Theresa Tedesco, Chief Business Correspondent, "Debt Ridden: The Story of the BCE Deal", *Financial Post*, September 27, 2008.

prerequisite for profitability. This mindset also blinded it to customers' needs; only Air Canada ranked above BCE in customer dissatisfaction.

BCE's bumbling reminded me of a skit from an American comedy series, Rowan & Martin's *Laugh In*, in which comedian Lily Tomlin plays a telephone operator. At one point she disconnects the phone service for a particular region and utters a now-famous quote:

"We don't care.

We don't have to.

We're the phone company."

In Play

When the merger negotiations with Telus fell through on June 30, 2007, it started the ball rolling. Now, the company was 'in play' and various private equity buyers circled their prey. They felt BCE was a good candidate for the disciplined rigour of private equity Eventually, the company accepted a bid of $42.75 per share in cash, for a total valuation of $51.7 billion from a group led by Teachers'. Up until that time, Teachers' was BCE's largest single shareholder with 6.3% of the stock. For years, along with everyone else, Teachers' had watched from the sidelines suffering through BCE's mismanagement. On several occasions, Teachers' had voiced its disapproval of management's failures.

Teachers' finally joined with an American consortium that included the private equity buyout firm, Providence Equity Partners, the world's leading PE firm focused on media, entertainment, communications and information. Providence, with $21 billion under management, was the best and sharpest investor in telecoms and capable of rationalizing BCE's operations.

Teachers' believed that BCE had a number of worthwhile holdings that Teachers' with a good PE firm could restructure. BCE was a healthy utility with strong cash flow. Although it was badly lagging its competitors and had a tarnished brand, the assets were still valuable and offered promise. To start, the workforce needed to be rationalized and BCE made more profitable.

On March 27, 2008 Canada's regulatory body, the Canada Radio-television and Telecommunications Commission (CRTC) approved the takeover, subject to conditions. Teachers' started to refocus the company immediately, not waiting for the deal to close. From the time the deal was approved until it fell through in November 2008, Teachers' had eight people working full-time on BCE. This is not an uncommon tactic in private equity. With so much riding on a deal, private equity buyers execute their game plan as early as possible. In this case, Teachers' was expected to write a cheque for $4 billion on closing.

At Teachers' initiative, BCE implemented a 100-day plan starting July, 2008 (even though Teachers' didn't yet own the company) to enhance its customer service, competitiveness and cost efficiency. BCE, notorious for having too many layers of management, reduced its management numbers by 15%. The goal was to sell non-core assets that didn't make sense and return BCE to its role as a communications service provider.

Teachers' identified three key growth areas in the telecoms sector: wireless, broadband and business communications and put a five-point strategy into effect: (1.) improve customer service, (2.) accelerate wireless, (3.) leverage landline momentum, (4.) invest in broadband networks and (5.) achieve a competitive cost structure.

The Bitter End

The deal was never consummated; it was signed in one economic era and due to close in another. The banks had agreed to an 18-month commitment in a turbulent market; too much leeway before closure. Meanwhile, the days of free-flowing money ended and a credit squeeze gripped the economy. Had the deal closed, the biggest losers would have been the banks.

Bankers are paid their bonuses based on fees from such deals. Anticipating large fees and sizeable bonuses, bankers bid aggressively to win the world's largest leveraged buyout. Their profit margins were razor thin and they underestimated the risks. While they awaited the deal's close, credit spreads collapsed such that the banks' cost of borrowing would have been much greater than the interest they received. The banks would have taken massive write-offs. One of those banks, Royal Bank of Scotland, subsequently collapsed and had to be rescued by the British government, and another, Citibank, needed U.S. government support, both largely because of poor risk management.

BCE's mismanagement was consistent to the end. Its board insisted on a 'solvency' condition that proved to be the deal's undoing and gave the private equity purchasers their way out. This condition provided that either the purchaser or BCE could walk away from the deal if BCE's independent auditors concluded that the value of BCE's assets would be less than its liabilities after the transaction took effect. If not for the 'solvency' condition, the purchasers would have borne significant costs owed to BCE in damages for backing out.

It is rare, if ever, for a seller to insert a 'solvency' condition. Perhaps the board could be forgiven for getting BCE's business model wrong in a rapidly changing telecoms environment, but how can it be excused for not structuring the transaction in the shareholders' best interests? This board included professionals with financial skill, such as investment banker and past chairman of RBC, Tony Fell, and celebrated entrepreneur, Jim Pattison.

As for the failed business model, board members had stellar credentials, but suffered from a lack of experience in BCE's own specialty. There was not a single name with expertise in telecoms. When the deal died on November 26th, 2008, the stock dropped to $22.03. It had gradually declined from its buyout price of $42.75 during the previous uncertain months. Overall, BCE's board and management had acted as both poor stewards of capital and managers of businesses.

Post Mortem

At the end, Teachers' left BCE as a re-energized company with a new management team. With Teachers' encouragement, George Cope was moved from the number two position to president and CEO, based on his wireless background. Also, at Teachers' urging, BCE removed excess layers of management and improved customer service. It was already working on growing BCE's wireless. To create a nimbler company, Teachers' set performance standards to benchmark BCE. George Cope is currently acting on Teachers' plan to revitalize BCE.

Would Teachers' have done a better job than the board and previous executives of BCE? We will never know, but Teachers' track record at the time was impressive. According to Jim Leech, head of Teachers', "Over the last 17 years (prior to the meltdown), (Teachers') Private Capital has returned more than 25% per annum."[30]

It is cases like BCE that caused frustration with publicly listed companies and led to the rise of private equity investing among pension funds and other large institutional investors. What BCE needed was a clear, concise strategy. Had BCE taken some of the money from the sale of assets and upgraded its network, pushed into wireless and returned excess money to shareholders, there would have been little need for private equity intervention. Instead, the company moved away from its core business and left shareholders holding the bag.

---

30. Arleen Jacobius, "Acquisition of BCE a 'Leverage-Lite' Buy", *Pensions & Investments*, July 9, 2007.

Some private equity strategies might have benefitted BCE. First, with private equity, the board of directors is more accountable to owners and there is a better alignment of interests. Members of the board often have sizeable portions of their own wealth invested in their portfolio businesses. Therefore, boards are focused and take the responsibility of ownership personally.

Michael Sabia did not return excess cash flow to investors and instead the money was squandered; unlike private equity where excess cash flow tends to be returned to investors.

While the multiples to be paid for BCE were high, they were not unmanageable for Teachers' and Providence which is one reason they succeeded in arranging favourable financing. The BCE deal was prudent for Teachers' and Providence. For Teachers' the risk was manageable and contained by the limited size of their equity participation. The excess risk was transferred to the banks that were prepared to lend against the value of BCE.

One lasting consequence of the potential deal is a decision by the Supreme Court of Canada on December 20th, 2008. The judgment was the result of an action by bondholders against BCE, claiming that they had been unfairly treated. The court ruled that, in takeovers, the company's board can do what is best for the corporation, and consider the interests of all stakeholders, including shareholders and bondholders.

In a takeover, such as BCE, the Canadian standard differs from the U.S.; Canada rejected the 'shareholder primacy' model where the interests of shareholders come first and the board's role is to maximize shareholder value. Acting with a view to "the best interests of the corporation", directors of a Canadian corporation could consider all stakeholders and are not obligated to equate the interests of the corporation only with the interests of the shareholders. This Canadian standard is built on "the corporation's duty as a responsible citizen" and acknowledges the corporation's social responsibility.[31]

It would have been interesting to see the result of a virtuoso team like Teachers' and Providence on both BCE's bottom line and long-term vision. This could have resulted in a fascinating study of public versus private equity. However, the story is not over and it is still possible that BCE and Teachers' will eventually return to the bargaining table.

---

31. For further details, see James C. Tory and John Cameron, *Torys on Mergers and Acquisitions – Directors Duties After BCE: Supreme Court of Canada Decides*, M&A 2009-2, January 9, 2009, <www.torys.com>.

THE MELTDOWN AND DROWNING IN DEBT

*"Leading up to the meltdown, institutions were
scrambling to get into private equity because of high
returns. Private equity firms were raising billions,
but the more the institutions gave you, the quicker
you had to spend it. The quicker you spent the money,
the quicker you could go back for more."*

Tony Melman, a Founding Partner,
Onex Corporation

My son is a partner in a successful Canadian private business. During the meltdown, I saw the fear in his eyes as he considered his business and reviewed his financial situation. I told him with confidence what I felt in my heart. Based on his youth, this was the best thing that could happen at his stage. This meltdown, would wring out the excesses of the last 10-15 years.

What were those excesses and how would they foretell a better future for private equity?

This book was started in a period of optimism and bridged the period through the meltdown, a period of disillusionment and despair. The timing allowed me to observe private equity at its best and its worst. Early in the book I reveled in the positive contributions of private equity. Now, as my book draws to its conclusion during a serious recession, it is time to dig deeper, summarize Canada's recent involvement and explore its future.

The 1980s

In the 1980s, founders of PE firms bought less-mature businesses. Businesses they bought had stable cash flow and they leveraged them slightly to enhance their value. The concept was to use businesses' own cash flow to finance purchases. The businesses were able to run themselves, while the founders paid down debt. Their goal was to sell them within 3-5 years, having earned a 20% annual return on their capital.

In Canada, these PE firms had the field to themselves. People didn't yet understand private equity and there were few PE firms. PE funds had not been created. Instead, the early partners went fund-raising for each individual business deal. I smiled when I learned that Onex, Canada's leading PE firm, had a staff consisting of three partners and two secretaries in the 1980s. What a rapid rise for a company with such a humble beginning!

The rules of engagement were conservative and straightforward. To buy a business, the firm put down at least 20%-25% of the purchase price. They paid no more than four times EBITDA and borrowed three times EBITDA. Back then, banks were tough lenders because banks that lent money held the debt until it was paid off. It is important to emphasize that the banks were risking their own capital. Eventually, this strategy changed and banks repackaged and resold the debt to others. This became one of the causes of the meltdown and current excesses.

Originally, firm partners generated their own deal flow and were responsible for a business until its sale. The role of the partner was both the acquisition and oversight of a business. Early professionals had banking or investment backgrounds and were capable of managing working capital, selling off over-valued assets, doing some strategic planning and adding operational efficiency. Because they stayed with a business until its sale they understood the business, even though their skills were largely financial and not managerial. This gradually changed as private equity grew, partners at a PE firm no longer stayed with their business throughout. They became too busy and their primary responsibility became finding the next deal.

The 1990s

As success in private equity evolved, it became an alternative asset class and PE firms changed their business model. They created PE funds. These were blind pools of capital that PE firms raised from investors to buy businesses in the future. Although there were restrictions on what they could buy, the days of raising money for specific deals were over. PE firms became asset managers. Fund-raising became more organized and consistent. The firms did more deals, more frequently, and raised bigger funds.

A successful PE firm's overhead expanded to accommodate this new complexity, creating larger professional organizations that needed to be fed. At this time the business model of 2 and 20 (2% fee on committed assets + 20% carried interest) was created in the U.S. and copied in Canada. To generate larger fees, successful firms needed to target larger-size deals, so their model changed from buying less mature businesses to owning mature businesses and buyouts of substantial public corporations.

Meanwhile the private equity industry became more competitive and it was no longer enough to fine tune a business and squeeze out unproductive assets. The investment thesis changed to 'let's do more with the business and grow the business'. The bigger the deals, the greater the fees, but how do you grow billion-dollar businesses that have already successfully penetrated their market and optimized their businesses? The private equity model was no longer simplistic, it required more strategizing and working with businesses.

The 21st Century

As the good times progressed, growth became artificial. More and more institutions and banks were clamoring to invest in private equity. This is when the big Canadian pensions became active. There was more demand to buy businesses, and banks were eager to lend. How much of the returns of the decade prior to the meltdown came from rising prices as opposed to genuine growth? To succeed, a PE firm was required to leverage more and spend more.

In the first decade of the 21st century, the biggest challenge for GPs became deal flow; finding deals and closing them. It was a whirligig of closings and moving on. If a GP completed a deal, he was expected to continue moving and finding the next. Less time was spent working with the business and developing strategies. Instead the GP assumed the role of 'foreman'. He went to see the business two days a month to determine if it was on track to achieve its returns.

In prior decades, these same professionals, who stayed with an investment, became so close to a business that they knew everything. Since they worked with fewer businesses, they were capable of transforming them. In the early 21st century, as they became more removed from their investment, the information GPs received was filtered through the board and its executives who were eager to please.

Leading up to the meltdown, there was not enough focus on improving the business; PE firms could count on higher prices and the debt that fueled them. Many PE firms moved away from their ideal of enhancing the performance of a business and relied on good times, increasing prices, and heavy leverage.

In this environment of perpetual deals, by 2006, structuring the financing became the number one concern in private equity. Banks were desperate to lend money and were offering debt greater than the value of the business. Deals done at 7-9 times EBITDA left little room for error. How could bankers have been so foolhardy? Banking had changed. Analogous to subprime behaviour in the U.S., instead of holding debt to maturity and relying on interest payments, banks could earn more from fees they received reselling debt. They became intermediaries. The worst excesses happened in the U.S. However, since most buyouts are North American or global, they impacted Canada as well.

Bankers received bonuses on the lucrative fees from arranging the financing. The safety of the bank's capital was no longer their responsibility. The game was about fees, syndication, repackaging and selling the debt. When banks approved a loan, their only concern became, 'what is the most we must retain to look respectable?' or 'how much of this debt can be sold to someone else?'

Currently there is a term that keeps cropping up. The term is moral hazard. Moral hazard refers to the care individuals take when they are personally liable for the consequences of their actions in contrast to their behaviour when someone else bears the consequences. When bankers were responsible for loans and the default risk, they behaved differently than when the loans could be passed on to someone else through syndications. Bankers became adept at playing 'hot potato' and moving debt out quickly. In a prior chapter, I described the dark side of private equity and the recent lax lending practices. There is one concept I saved for last: 'stapled debt'.

Stapled Debt

Large businesses on the verge of a sale would approach an M&A specialist who gave advice and arranged an auction. The biggest and most sophisticated M&A divisions were attached to their banks or to investment dealers. Initially, these M&A firms only managed the sale process and were paid a fee based on the sale price. As the market became hot, M&A advisors associated with banks started to attach a financing package to the deal. This was known as 'stapled debt' because the buyer knew ahead of time what could be borrowed.

For the buyer, this provided the reassurance of receiving favourable financing. For competing banks who coveted the lucrative financing fees, it caused a feeding frenzy. Often the result was a bidding war among competing banks offering better terms. Banks tripped all over each other to win the riskiest most high profile deals. Meanwhile, prices of businesses were forced up because the cost of financing became cheaper.

Sadly, this is not always in the best interests of the business. If there is too much debt, buyers must starve the business and prioritize debt payment. With so much debt, the GP can't afford to optimize the business to make it saleable. Currently many PE funds are saddled with businesses for which they paid too much and which were over-leveraged. With the market falling, getting out of over-priced businesses will be slow. As business deteriorates, the businesses with aggressive financing are at greater risk of going under, as are the banks that financed them.

In their PE funds, GPs will face write-downs on poorly performing investments. LPs looking at their portfolios will be reluctant to honor their future drawdowns. My guess is that they will forfeit investments instead of throwing good money after bad. Investors who borrowed to make commitments to these funds may not respond to capital calls as they struggle with their own cash flow problems. This means some businesses will not receive their funding.

In 'hot potato' banking, money changes hands rapidly, increasing the flow of capital. Now the reverse is happening as the flow diminishes. Currently, the world is deleveraging. With a shortage of capital, demand has dropped. Ultimately, this will lead to lower prices and better value as only the best businesses will survive. At that point, the excesses of the past decade will have been wrung out.

THE COMING AGE OF INTELLIGENT CAPITAL

*"With markets and businesses blowing up all around
them, buyout firms calmly made their case to big
investors that they were still worthy stewards of capital.
In 2008 they attracted $554 billion from pension funds,
university endowments and other big investors,
down only modestly from the record $625 billion
the previous year."*

Peter Carbonara and Jessica Silver-Greenberg,
"How Private Equity Could Revive the Economy,"
Businessweek, May 18, 2009

There is a good chance that the meltdown of 2008 will usher in a new period driven by the intelligent use of capital. After the recession, investors will become more selective and expectations will be lowered. Instead of chasing excessive rates of return, PE firms might be satisfied with lower returns commensurate with less risk. The exceptional returns of the past, in excess of 20%, may be unattainable. Even expectations of 20% could drop; perhaps 10-15% will suffice. The overemphasis on doing deals and exploiting leverage will subside. In an environment where capital, credit and higher exit prices are harder to come by, PE firms will need to change their models.

The heady days of quick decisions and success belonging to the highest bidder will subside in the foreseeable future. PE firms will be forced to use less leverage as bank borrowing becomes less dependable. At the same time, firms will need to hold larger reserves of contingency capital to support businesses that fail to meet their targets. More equity tied up in a business because of decreased leverage will result in reduced percentage returns on invested capital.

Realizing cash flow will be tougher than ever, PE firms will be obliged to wait for better times in order to recapitalize their portfolio businesses and take money out. In a fund, the hold time before a company can be sold and money returned to investors could become longer.

On the positive side, with the collapse of corporate America, there will be great buys. PE funds that must exit their portfolio companies will be forced to accept lower prices. Prices paid could go below the 4X EBITDA paid during the 1980s in the early days of Canadian private equity; certainly well below the 8-9X EBITDA of 2006. A few pundits predict prices as low as 3X EBITDA. Meanwhile, PE firms that stay afloat will need to have available cash or the ability to raise new pools of capital from investors.

To survive, PE firms will need justifiable assumptions for businesses it buys. Exit strategies will assume a greater priority and portfolio businesses will be bought with better plans for business development. The focus will shift towards optimizing businesses and growing them as opposed to financial engineering.

We might see a return to buying smaller businesses where PE firms can have a greater impact. With less mature businesses, firms are capable of implementing multi-dimensional growth strategies to improve management, products and/or distribution. In contrast, in a large mature business, its potential has been optimized and a PE firm becomes subject to the law of diminishing returns. The bigger and more expensive the business the smaller the options for adding value.

In a contracting economy, PE firms might reexamine their own business models in order to differentiate themselves from their rivals. To stay competitive, PE firms will become more sophisticated and develop distinctive areas of expertise. There is already a trend towards organizational changes among some PE firms. Top performing PE firms, capable of consistently generating above average rates of return regardless of PE firm size, deal size, or geographic diversification, are setting the standards.

Three factors stand out as worthy of emulation. Superior PE firms are capable of the following: targeting better deals, bidding more accurately and finally transforming their portfolio businesses.[32]

Targeting better deals. Firstly, PE firms that succeed usually focus on a single industry, subset of industries or type of business. Such firms go the extra mile to become insiders in their sector. Partners include not just investment bankers or dealmakers but industry experts. These firms are well-connected industry players and therefore quick at pinpointing opportunities. Their expertise earns them the confidence and respect of business executives and they can actively network within their domain. As insiders, they have the advantage of seeing deals early and finding untapped value.

Bidding more accurately. Secondly, insider firms have 'information intelligence'. In other words, they have detailed knowledge of their industry that allows them to foresee trends. This is a great advantage when it comes to evaluating business potential. At times, it allows PE firms to bid aggressively whereas at other times to be more cautious.

---

32. Heino Meerkatt, John Rose and Michael Brigl, *The Advantage of Persistence, How the Best Private-Equity Firms "Beat the Fade"*, The Boston Consulting Group, February, 2008.

Transforming portfolio businesses. Finally, the best PE firms have improved capabilities to optimize businesses. They include partners with consulting or operational backgrounds. A partner with an operating background can set up comprehensive benchmarking of a company in order to compare it to its peers and measure its performance against its industry. It is difficult for a PE firm to implement change without disrupting a business. However, individuals with managerial experience can make subtle changes without putting excessive pressure on the existing organization.

This will be a tall order for the average PE firm organized along traditional lines where emphasis was on deal-making and fundraising. Many PE firms attempt to meet these three objectives, but the firms that have gone the farthest in implementing a value creation model have been the most successful.[33] Top quartile funds that have consistently produced the best investment returns are a product of PE firms that have adopted this focus.

In the past, the biggest barrier to entry for a PE firm was finding 'cash'. PE firms were run by investment bankers adept at fundraising. It became obvious during the meltdown that cash was merely a commodity and that successful PE firms needed a greater range of capabilities.

As a result of the slower environment there will be consolidation among PE firms. Those able to identify their competitive advantage may become the industry leaders of the future. Leading firms will target niches and know them thoroughly. This will create a divergence between specialist PE firms and generalists. In Canada, the focus will return to home-grown businesses and baby boomers selling their businesses.

2010 and Beyond

In the Canadian private equity environment, an important trend will be the retirement of the baby boomers. The first baby boomers turn 65 in 2011 and it is anticipated that 50% of them will retire over the next ten years. The current crisis will drive this trend. Many are devastated by the meltdown and will reexamine their appetite for risk. Stress levels may precipitate decisions by the end of 2009. It is estimated that approximately 20,000 businesses will be for sale in Canada over the next 10 years. Of these, 100 businesses a year will be of decent size. The majority of Canada's private businesses are expected to be sold by baby boomers in the coming decade.

---

33. Heino Meerkatt, John Rose and Michael Brigl, *The Advantage of Persistence, How the Best Private-Equity Firms "Beat the Fade"*, The Boston Consulting Group, February, 2008.

Just as PE firms mispriced risk prior to the meltdown, so did business owners. Owners were drawing substantial sums out of their businesses and appraised their companies by what they could put in their pocket after tax, not necessarily by what the market would pay. Negotiating with them was challenging and so businesses were expensive to buy.

Owners felt there was no point selling if they weren't paid enough to replace their business income on an after tax sale. This slower economy will come as a reality check. Many will realize that they do not have a succession plan and need a better handle on their own exit plan. Prices for their businesses will drop in line with market conditions. This will create better opportunities for PE firms.

Because Canada is made up of small, diverse, regional businesses, many businesses are run by one or two people over-burdened by the current pressure and stress levels. Often middle management has not been trained to assume responsibility.

Despite the assumptions regarding family businesses, in most cases, the children don't want the business even though it may be successful and profitable. Most kids are neither suitable nor trained to take over. The kids have been silver-spooned and schooled and moved on to professions or careers of their own. Over 70 per cent of family-owned companies do not survive the transition from founder to second generation. Therefore, PE firms will assume even greater significance.

Perhaps the retirement of the baby boomers will be a catalyst for change. The Canadian way for businesses was to stay small and nimble. There seemed little drive to become bigger. This style does not need to be maintained. Currently, Canadian businesses seem to plateau at $50 million in enterprise value, but businesses could be made bigger. PE firms are capable of consolidating businesses and creating a bigger vision. PE Firms can make acquisitions to build more efficient businesses. It is not easy finding businesses that can be merged and the logistics of combining them can be complicated. Nevertheless, that is the skill that PE firms often take pride in; the ability to spot trends and build greater enterprises.

Changing of the Guard

For larger Canadian businesses over $100 million in enterprise value, there are no geographical borders. They will find interested PE firms as purchasers anywhere in North America and abroad. However, PE firms in Canada are shaped by our business environment. These firms would starve waiting for $100 million deals here. Although we have public sector pension plans capable of acting as PE firms, buying and overseeing major businesses well in excess of this amount, the majority of our PE firms are small and perceived as part of a 'Mom and Pop' industry. The coming decade may create an opportunity for the growth of small Canadian PE firms.

Local PE firms have unique advantages for small business. The firms' GPs know their marketplace. For example, they have better local banking relationships vital for the expansion of small businesses. With cash sparse, Canadian PE firms will evolve to transition large numbers of businesses as founders retire. Smaller businesses require more time and effort after a change of ownership. In the current slow environment these demands can only increase.

To accommodate retiring business owners, PE firms might become more flexible. In the past, most PE firms insisted on control and wouldn't consider buying less than 66% of a business. This allowed a PE firm to take almost any action at will, including selling the business. With less available cash, perhaps taking a minority interest will become acceptable with legal clauses that offer some control and more protection.

For business owners, selling minority interests allows them to gradually work their way out of a business. Meanwhile, PE firms have more time to adapt and manage the owners' exit. Going forward, the expertise offered by private equity will be vital in moving business from one generation to the next. PE firms bring rigour, process and time lines to a business that aid the transitioning process.

Most importantly, retirement is not always about money. Many baby boomers want their legacy to survive. They want their business to continue for the sake of their employees, management and communities. Some want the business to continue to grow. For those who want to ensure that the business remains in Canada, that it stays independent and that employees retain their jobs, selling to a Canadian PE firm offers greater assurance.

"The End of the Beginning"[34]

As I write this at the nadir of the meltdown, many articles predict the end of the private equity industry. They claim the industry was a flash in the pan; a

---

34. Winston Churchill, *The End of the Beginning*, The Lord Mayor's Luncheon, Mansion House, November 10, 1942.

result of too much easy credit. They argue that venture capital will always be needed to seed new businesses at an early development stage, but buyouts and the industry as a whole will start to dwindle.

I found these predictions frivolous. Private equity added efficiency to our market system. It was an alternative to public markets and brought with it new and improved ways of governing businesses. Some of its strategies were ultimately incorporated into public companies. The strength of a market economy is competition and the competition that private equity brought to public companies forced them to reexamine their methods and face their shortcomings.

In Canada, a public company like BCE was a case in point. After years of disappointing its shareholders, it was put in play by private equity syndicates and forced to face its arrogance and mismanagement. With the specter of private equity hanging over it, a public corporation cannot remain insular and hide from obligations to its shareholders.

I came across a survey showing that large numbers of CEOs are attracted to private equity as a career choice. About 78% felt that leading a private equity-backed company is a better career option than running a publicly owned business.[35] This is not surprising. Private companies can offer better opportunities for creativity and less bureaucracy. Whenever I mention that I am writing a book about private equity, my most enthusiastic fans are young financial professionals who wonder about the industry and its prospects.

For all the hype and excitement that surrounded the industry worldwide over the last decade, private equity assets, though sizeable in dollar value, are little more than a drop in the bucket. Buyouts represented a mere 3% of the total market capitalization of world stock markets (approximately $2 trillion out of $60 trillion). Thus, there is vast potential for it to expand in the future.

Private equity is only at the 'end of the beginning'. In the recent past, the availability of excessive credit gave private equity a leg up. Going forward, the bonanza of exorbitant leverage is over, but the industry will remain because it often out-performed public equities and succeeded in delivering good results. Therefore, in my view, the private equity industry will continue to evolve during this period of reckoning and its future remains rosy. In the coming age of intelligent capital, PE firms will have to spend money wisely and add value to portfolio businesses in order to earn their profit and navigate through harder times.

---

35. <www.privateequitywire.co.uk>, December 23, 2008.

APPENDIX

TAX AND LEGAL ISSUES

TAX ISSUES IN CANADIAN PE FUNDS

By Jocelyn Blanchet
Partner, Deloitte & Touche LLP

Most investors in private equity would typically invest in this asset class by making an investment in a private equity fund, rather than investing directly in private companies. A private equity fund is akin to a mutual fund; it is a pool of capital that is professionally managed by a fund "sponsor" or management team that provides the necessary skill and expertise to generate positive returns.

As discussed in the chapter on legal considerations for investments in private equity, private equity funds are generally structured as limited partnerships. In this way, they are different than most mutual funds (which are generally established as mutual fund trusts or mutual fund corporations) and are, therefore, treated differently for income tax purposes. This chapter describes the income tax considerations associated with making an investment in a private equity fund. This chapter considers the tax consequences associated with investments in Canadian-based private equity funds or, more specifically, in a private equity fund that is formed in Canada and that has a management team located in Canada. Although some Canadians may choose to invest in a private equity fund established in the United States (or in another country), or that is managed by a non-Canadian investment team, the tax consequences associated with such investments are generally much more complicated and beyond the scope of this book.

Fund Taxation

In Canada, limited partnerships are "flow-through" vehicles. That is, they are generally not required to pay any income tax but rather calculate their income for tax purposes as though they were a separate person and allocate or "flow through" this income or loss to the investors. Such income is allocated pursuant to the terms of the limited partnership agreement and is generally based on each investor's commitment relative to total fund commitments, after taking into account allocations or distributions to the fund sponsor (including distributions in respect of the carried interest). The investors include this allocation in their income for tax purposes when preparing their own tax returns and are liable to pay income tax on these amounts.

The income or loss of the fund for tax purposes must be allocated to the investors irrespective of whether the investors have received any distributions from the fund during the year. Accordingly, there are many circumstances in which investors may be allocated items of income for tax purposes without receiving corresponding distributions. For example, the fund may earn income that is not paid in cash or that is illiquid and cannot be distributed, or the fund may use income earned to reinvest in fund assets rather than making distributions to investors (particularly during the Commitment Period). Investors in private equity funds should be cognizant that they may be allocated income for tax purposes without corresponding cash distributions and that the income taxes payable on these amounts will need to be funded from other sources.

Income allocated by the limited partnership is generally treated in the same way as similar income earned by the investor directly. For example, dividends received by the partnership from Canadian-resident corporations and allocated to investors are treated as Canadian dividends to the investors. Because of the nature of the private equity fund's activities, the income allocated would typically consist of dividends, interest income, and capital gains from the sale of investments. Many funds generate losses for tax purposes in the initial years because management fees paid to the fund sponsor or manager can exceed income generated by the fund in these initial years. In addition, dividends from Canadian corporations and capital gains are subject to preferential tax treatment to Canadian-resident investors and subject to lower rates of income tax.

Some private equity funds invest in businesses that are themselves structured as limited partnerships. This is an efficient method of investing because the profits generated by these businesses are not subject to corporate income tax and are allocated directly to the fund (and, ultimately, to the fund's investors); in short, the income of the business is subject to only a single layer of tax (the tax levied on the fund's investors). As with other types of income earned by the fund, such business income would be allocated to each of the fund's investors for income tax purposes and would be subject to income tax at the rates applicable to business income, irrespective of whether or not the profits are distributed to the investors. Such rates will depend on the provinces in which the business operates since business income is generally subject to income tax in the province in which such income was earned (unlike investment income which may be subject to the income tax rates of the investor's province of residence or head office).

Because income may be allocated without corresponding distributions, and because the amount of income to be allocated could depend on the profits of underlying businesses, it can be difficult for investors to predict the annual income tax liabilities associated with an investment in a private equity fund until the annual tax reporting is completed by the fund.

Generally speaking, however, the tax reporting and allocation process is simple for investors. The fund will generally prepare tax information slips (referred to as T5013 slips) detailing the amount and nature of income allocated to each individual investor. These slips are similar in nature to the T4 and T5 slips issued to individuals to report employment and investment income, respectively. Such slips must generally be prepared and filed by the fund no later than March 31 of the following calendar year.

Because Canadian private equity funds invest in private companies, capital gains realized and allocated by such funds may qualify for the lifetime capital gains exemption. Residents of Canada are generally entitled to a deduction that exempts from tax $750,000 of capital gains realized on the disposition of certain qualifying shares. Such qualifying assets generally include shares of Canadian-based private corporations that carry on an active business principally within Canada.

Ceasing Residency

Investors that cease to be resident in Canada may be forced to sell their interest in the fund because of the impact that this change in residency can have on other investors in the fund. Where a single investor in a particular fund is a non-resident of Canada (even if that investor has made only a very modest commitment), the entire limited partnership is viewed as a non-resident of Canada for Canadian income tax purposes, subjecting all payments made to the fund by Canadian residents to withholding tax. Accordingly, fund sponsors will often adopt mechanisms, including "forced sale" provisions in the limited partnership agreement for the fund, to ensure that the investors in the fund are all resident in Canada for tax purposes.

How to Purchase

Tax considerations associated with a fund investment will also impact how the investment will be made, including which person or entity within a family unit will make the investment. An investment in a limited partnership is generally not an eligible asset for a registered retirement savings plan (RRSP) or for the tax-free savings account (TFSA). Accordingly, the investment will need to be made in a taxable account. However, the taxable account may belong to a spouse, family trust, or personal holding corporation.

Tax considerations will impact which person or entity in the family unit will make the investment. For example, the investor would ideally be able to make use of any losses allocated by the Fund in the initial years and should, therefore, have other sources of taxable income. In addition, consideration should be given to whether any members of the family are able to benefit from the lifetime capital gains exemption on capital gains allocated by the Fund.

When deciding which entity will make the investment, it is also important to ensure that investor has the financial resources to be able to satisfy the entire Commitment. As described in the chapter on legal considerations, most limited partnership agreements provide for significant adverse economic implications if a particular investor is not able to satisfy their Commitment when the funds are called.

Conclusion

Because private equity funds are typically structured as limited partnerships which are flow-through vehicles for income tax purposes, the fund investment will likely be made in a taxable account and returns will generally be taxed in the same manner as other investment income earned directly by the investor. Furthermore, the tax reporting associated with such investments should generally be relatively straightforward since such income is reported on a tax slip prepared by the fund manager or administrator and issued to the investor.

However, when making an investment in a private equity fund, investors should be cognizant of the income tax consequences associated with such an investment including, in particular, that income may be allocated to the investor for income tax purposes even if no distributions are made to the investor. Investors should ensure that they have sufficient financial resources to fund the tax liabilities arising as a result of such allocations.

LEGAL ISSUES IN CANADIAN PE FUNDS

By Cameron Koziskie
Partner, Torys LLP

A decision to invest in a private equity fund is a significant economic and legal commitment that must be carefully planned, reviewed and executed. A necessary first step in that process is to obtain a solid understanding of the basic legal underpinnings—as well as the jargon—of a private equity fund and the fundraising process. Once armed with this understanding, you, as the investor, can make educated decisions.

The decision-making process should involve the advice of skilled lawyers familiar with private equity funds. These lawyers can assist with the evaluation and structuring of the investment and ensure that you understand your rights and responsibilities. The purpose of this chapter is to give you an understanding of the basics so that you can develop a list of some key questions to ask your advisors as you embark on investing in a private equity fund.

Fund Creation and Documentation

A private equity fund is set up by the management team of the fund (also called the "sponsors"[36]). The fund is typically structured as a limited partnership between the sponsors and the investors (who are also called "limited partners") because this form of organization is both simple and tax efficient.

The sponsors spend months laying the groundwork for the launch of the fund. Much of this time is spent identifying potential investors and making pitches for their support. In the background, the sponsors' lawyers are drafting numerous documents needed to organize the fund and permit the fundraising. The key documents include an offering memorandum, a limited partnership agreement and a subscription agreement.

The offering memorandum provides a basic overview of the fund and related matters. It functions primarily as a marketing document to entice investors to invest in the fund; however, it can provide a wealth of useful information

---

36. The management team of the fund will often hold their interest in the fund through a complex structure involving many separate special purpose corporations. For example, it is common for one corporation controlled by the management team to be the general partner of the fund, and a separate corporation, also controlled by the management team, to be the manager of the fund. For simplicity in this chapter, we use the term "sponsors" to refer generically to the management team and the group of entities they control that are involved in the fund.

to potential investors, including detailed descriptions of the management team, their prior experience in private equity, the strategy of the fund, the principal terms of the fund and the risk factors applicable to the fund. It is important to note that an offering memorandum is *not* a prospectus and, therefore, investors are not provided with the same level of legal protection as given in a prospectus offering of a public company. Investors resident in some provinces may, however, have some legal protections if the offering memorandum contains a misrepresentation.

The limited partnership agreement, which often runs more than 100 pages, contains the comprehensive description of the relationship between the sponsors on the one hand and the investors on the other. It is the most important legal document of the investment transaction and therefore warrants much attention in the decision to invest. The subscription agreement is also important because it sets out the basis on which the fund will accept you as an investor.

Key Features of the Fund

The fund documentation will set out the terms and conditions of the fund. Some common features that will be described in the fund documentation include the following:

- Investor Commitment
  - Each investor subscribes for limited partnership units of the fund and agrees to make a specified commitment of capital to the fund. The commitment establishes the maximum amount that the investor wants to invest over the life of the fund. The fund draws down that capital from time to time to make investments or to pay fund expenses by issuing "capital call notices" to the investors. Upon receiving a capital call notice, the investors have a short period (often five to ten days) in which to fund their proportionate share of the amount drawn down by the fund.
  - The fund typically has a "commitment period" (also called an "investment period") during which the fund can make new investments. This period can range from three to six years. After the end of the commitment period, there is a "harvesting period" during which the fund cannot make new investments, but can only make "follow-on" investments into portfolio companies already owned by the fund. During the harvesting period, which typically lasts a further three to six years, the sponsors manage and divest the fund's investments. If the fund has not disposed of all of its investments by the end of the harvesting period, the limited partnership

agreement often forces the liquidation and windup of the fund subject to any extension periods that are available.

- Economic Provisions (Fees, Expenses and Carried Interest)

  - The fund is typically responsible for all the expenses incurred to source, acquire, manage and dispose of investments, including the expenses related to deals that are not completed ("broken deals"). The investors effectively fund these expenses as the fund draws upon capital from the investors to pay these expenses. The investors will get this money back if the fund is ultimately profitable.

  - The fund pays an annual management fee to the sponsors, often 2% of committed capital throughout the investment period and 1.5% of invested capital throughout the harvesting period. Similar to costs noted above, the investors effectively fund this fee, but they will get this money back if the fund is ultimately profitable.

  - The sponsors and the investors will split the profits of the fund according to a formula set out in the limited partnership agreement. The amount received by the sponsors is called the "carried interest" and is often set at 20% of net realized profits.

  - Most funds are structured so that the carried interest is payable to the sponsors only after a hurdle return is met. In many funds, the hurdle return is set at 8% per annum. Under this structure, investors receive a return of their capital contributions (sometimes all capital contributions, sometimes contributions relating only to realized investments of the fund), and then a hurdle return equal to 8% per annum on their contributed and returned capital. After the hurdle return has been satisfied, distributions are made to the sponsors so they can "catch up" and receive 20% of the amounts distributed to the investors under the hurdle return and to the sponsors under their catch-up payment. After that, the sponsors and the limited partners simply share profits so that 80% of the overall profits go to the investors and 20% to the sponsors.

  - As an investor, you will often hear the terms "2 and 20" or "20 over 8." Those terms are jargon to describe the fees and expenses of the fund. "2 and 20" means that the sponsors charge a management fee during the investment period consisting of 2% of commitments and the sponsors earn a 20% carried interest. "20 over 8" provides a bit more detail regarding the carried interest—namely, that the 20% carried interest is payable only after an 8% hurdle return is achieved.

163

- A "fund of funds" is a private equity fund which invests in a number of underlying private equity funds. If you are investing in a "fund of funds," there is some duplication of fees, because the fund of funds charges a management fee and a carried interest and each of the underlying private equity funds that the fund of funds invests in also charges a management fee and a carried interest.

- The section of the limited partnership agreement that describes the return of capital and division of profits between the investors and the sponsors is commonly referred to as the "Distribution Waterfall." As you would expect, much thought goes into that provision to ensure that it captures the intended economic deal between the investors and the sponsors. No single formulation of the Distribution Waterfall fits all funds—in fact, dozens of variations and permutations are possible. A skilled lawyer will be able to help you navigate the subtleties.

The Investment Process: Becoming a Limited Partner

It is common for an investor to be required to sign a subscription agreement in which he or she makes numerous representations and warranties. These representations and warranties are often very detailed and include matters such as the authorization and enforceability of the fund documentation, the application of various securities law exemptions and the investor's compliance with laws related to money laundering and terrorism. You should review the subscription agreement carefully.

Since the capital commitments of the investors are to be drawn down over time, the sponsors of the fund need to ensure that each limited partner has sufficient assets to satisfy capital calls. If an investor is a holding company, the fund may seek assurances from the controlling shareholders (like a guarantee or a comfort letter) that the holding company will have sufficient funds to cover its full capital commitment.

Once you have confirmed your interest in the fund, you will typically receive the package of legal documents needed to implement your investment in the fund. As noted above, these legal documents will have been prepared by the sponsors' lawyers. Typically, only the two or three largest investors in a fund will have enough clout (i.e., commit a sufficiently large amount to the fund) to convince the sponsors to accept changes to the terms in the documents. All the other investors will be effectively told to "take it or leave it." Given this dynamic, it is still worthwhile to have your own lawyers review the documentation to ensure that you know what you are getting into. In some circumstances, a number of "small" investors may be able to join forces and retain one lawyer to represent them. This approach streamlines the process, minimizes costs to the investors and, depending on the circumstances, may allow that group to have enough clout to convince the sponsors to accept some of their changes.

The fundraising process is long and arduous for the sponsors. It is very common for funds to have multiple closings. In essence, once a critical mass of investors has been lined up, the fund will complete a first closing and get the first wave of investors signed up and committed to the fund. After the early investors are signed up, the sponsors may continue for a period of time—often as long as one year—to beat the bushes to find additional investors. If additional investors are found, they then join the fund at a second or later closing. If no additional investors come in, the fund carries on with only the commitments of the first-closing investors. Investors who join the fund at a later date will typically pay management fees and participate in all investments as if they were limited partners on the first closing date of the fund.

Key Legal Questions

With this backdrop of the basics of a private equity fund, let us now turn to a list of a few key legal considerations. This checklist represents some of the main issues you should be discussing with your lawyer before committing to the fund.

1. What is my total economic exposure to the fund?

As noted above, in your subscription agreement and in the limited partnership agreement you commit to invest a specified dollar amount in the fund, and that dollar amount can be drawn upon by the fund from time to time. In most circumstances, that amount is the maximum of your total economic exposure to the fund. A secondary question is what happens to your economic exposure after you have received some capital back and/or received a distribution of profits from the fund. Many provinces have statutory requirements that obligate an investor who has received distributions of capital and/or profits from a fund to return those amounts to the fund in certain circumstances (for example, if the fund shortly thereafter discovers liabilities that it cannot pay). In addition, the limited partnership agreements of some funds impose contractual requirements to return capital to the fund in certain circumstances, either to be used to make new investments or to pay fund expenses (often referred to as "recycling" or "reinvestment") or to be used to satisfy certain obligations of the fund (often referred to as the "LP giveback provisions").

2. Tell me about "limited liability protections" and what I need to be concerned about.

Most limited partnership statutes distinguish between "limited partners" and "general partners." General partners control the partnership and make all decisions affecting the partnership; limited partners are intended to be merely passive investors. The additional powers given to general partners come at a cost: by statute, the general partner is personally responsible for all the debts and liabilities of the partnership (this is the reason why in most circumstances, the general partner is in fact a shell corporation). Limited partners, however, are given protection by statute and are not responsible for the debts and liabilities of the partnership (limited partners are thus afforded the protection similar to that of a shareholder of a corporation).

As a general rule, a limited partner is protected only if the partner does not participate in the business and affairs of the fund. It is therefore very important to ensure that you, as a limited partner, always conduct yourself with this restriction in mind. Your lawyer should be able to advise you on the risks that may arise, given your expected involvement with the fund. In most situations, the analysis is easy since the investor truly is passive, with no role in the fund.

Some situations, however, are more complex and require detailed review—for example, if you become a member of the fund's Advisory Committee, you should be careful to ensure that the powers of the Advisory Committee do not extend to making the committee members participate in the business and affairs of the fund. It is worth noting that certain provinces provide better legal protection for limited partners than others. Your lawyer should be able to advise whether the province chosen by the fund will be helpful or unhelpful in limiting your liability for the debts and liabilities of the fund.

3. Tell me about public disclosure and confidentiality.

Although private equity investments may seem "private," be prepared for some limited public disclosure of basic information about the investors. Most provinces require public disclosure of the name, address and capital commitment of each investor. The fund, on the other hand, expects confidentiality from all investors and will impose strict confidentiality covenants on the investors to protect the sensitive information about the fund and the underlying portfolio companies in which the fund invests. As an investor, you will also want to determine whether the limited partnership agreement imposes any restrictions on your ability to carry on competitive businesses. Most funds, in fact, recognize the passive role of the investors and specify the exact opposite (i.e., that no investor is restricted in any way and the investors need not account to the fund for any profits earned in any other business enterprise or undertaking). Look for that type of confirmation for your own protection.

4. Tell me about my other main rights and obligations.

The limited partnership agreement imposes a number of restrictions on the investors. These are some of the key ones to consider:

- Private equity investors are often subject to numerous restrictions on transferring ownership in a fund to another investor, including a requirement to get the consent of the sponsors before any proposed transfer (which consent may be given or withheld for any reason). In addition, various securities laws will restrict transfer. These restrictions may make it very difficult to sell your ownership in a private equity fund.

- Serious consequences will result if an investor defaults in making a capital contribution when requested by the fund (for example, one common consequence to such a default is a forced sale of your interest in the fund at the lesser of (i) the fair market value of the units at the date of default; and (ii) 50% of the amount contributed to the fund to date). Make sure you understand the consequences and, to avoid them, take your capital commitment very seriously.

- It is common for the limited partnership agreement to provide that the sponsors and a specified majority of the investors (i.e., those holding a majority or two-thirds of the capital commitments) may amend the limited partnership agreement. Consider this provision carefully and determine if your interest is adequately protected.

Conclusion

The legal aspects of an investment in a private equity fund are intricate and the details are tremendously important. By understanding the legal framework of a private equity fund and your rights and obligations, you and your lawyer will be able to make informed decisions about private equity fund investing and this can set the framework for a successful private equity investment.

GLOSSARY

Assets Under Management

The value of investments managed by a PE fund.

Buyouts

Purchase of majority ownership in a business. As these businesses generate regular cash flow, debt is used for their acquisition.

The Carry or Carried Interest

A share of the profits that GPs receive after the LP's capital has been returned (usually 20%).

Due Diligence

The process of assessing the financial viability and profit potential of a target investment by reviewing the operational, legal, accounting, tax and other information relating to the target business.

EBITDA

This acronym signifies earnings before interest, taxes, depreciation and amortization. A measurement used to determine the operating cash flow of a business and to assess its value.

Enterprise Value

The estimated price at which a business may be sold.

Fund of Funds (FOF)

A fund that holds a portfolio of other PE funds rather than investing in private businesses directly. Its objective is to give investors broader diversification and asset allocation. To provide this service, an FOF adds an extra layer of fees.

General Partner (GP)

GPs make all decisions relating to the PE fund, and thus oversee the purchase, monitor and sell businesses on behalf of a PE fund.

Hurdle

The minimum return that must be exceeded before the GP is entitled to a share of the profits.

Institutional Investors

These are the most frequent investors in private equity and consist of pension funds, insurance companies, university endowments and charitable foundations.

Leveraged Buyout

The purchase of a company by using debt, with the company's assets as collateral.

Limited Partner (LP)

An LP is an investor in a PE fund but is not involved in making decisions on the investments. Institutional investors are the most frequent LPs.

Limited Partnership Agreement

This is the contract that defines the relationship between the GPs and LPs and outlines the rights, obligations and restrictions of each.

Management Fee

A fee charged by the GP or an affiliate for managing a fund. The fee is intended to cover the manager's on-going expenses such as salaries, rent and overhead (usually 2%).

Multiple

A ratio used to assess the purchase price of a private business. The ratio is a multiplier normally based on EBITDA.

Portfolio Company

A business owned by a PE fund.

Private Equity

Ownership in a business that is not listed on a stock exchange.

Private Equity Firm (PE firm)

A professional management company that invests in private businesses through pools of capital called PE funds. The PE firm oversees these investments (portfolio companies), until they are sold (or exited).

Private Equity Fund (PE fund)

Blind pools of capital that are raised from investors to buy businesses in the future. Most PE funds are structured as limited partnerships. Investments are held for a maximum time period, usually 10-12 years, after which the fund is wound up.

Venture

A minority investment in a new or young business, usually in a promising new sector, such as information technology or biotechnology. As companies at this stage have insufficient cash flow, they cannot obtain debt financing.

Vintage Year

The year in which a PE fund was started.

ACKNOWLEDGEMENTS

Special Thanks

> To Dr. Bruce Pomeranz: my Harvard-graduate scientist and husband/ editor who insisted on clarity whenever I would succumb to poetry.

> To Ian Campbell Ferguson Rodger, past news editor, Financial Times, London, for his excellent editing and mentoring in the art of writing.

> To the following three professionals who read the draft for accuracy and professionalism: Jocelyn Blanchet, Partner, Deloitte & Touche LLP; Cameron D. Koziskie, Partner, Torys LLP; Andrew Brenton, CEO, Turtle Creek Asset Management Inc.

Interviewees

I sincerely thank the following professionals, many of them leaders in the private equity field, for the generous gift of their time and especially their honest assessment and profound insights into the industry. Despite hectic schedules they made themselves available for interviews and follow-ups and were prepared to tackle controversial issues. This book would not have been possible without them.

Most of the knowledge gleaned from the interviews was interspersed throughout the book. Only eight conversations were quoted at length to illustrate certain aspects of the industry.

Institutional Investors

> Claude Lamoureux, Past President and CEO, Ontario Teachers' Pension Plan

> Jim Leech, President and CEO, Ontario Teachers' Pension Plan

> Joncarlo Mark, Senior Portfolio Manager, CalPERS

Don J. Morrison, Senior Vice President, OMERS Capital Partners

Ed Rieckelman, Alberta Investment Management Corp.

Mark D. Wiseman, Senior Vice President, Private Investments, Canada Pension Plan Investment Board

Private Equity Firms

Jim Ambrose, The Shotgun Fund, Argosy Partners

Chris Arsenault, Managing Partner, iNovia Capital Inc.

Marc Beauchamp, President and Managing Partner, Novacap

Brent S. Belzberg, Senior Managing Partner, Torquest Partners

Cody Church, Managing Director, TriWest Capital Partners

Thomas R. Kennedy, Partner, Kensington Capital

Elmer Kim, Managing Director, Whitecastle Private Equity Partners

Michael Lay, Managing Partner, ONCAP Management Partners

John B. MacIntyre, Birch Hill Equity Partners

Don McLauchlin, Vice-President, Roynat Capital

Tony Melman, a Founding Partner of Onex Corporation

Jeff Parr, Co-CEO and Managing Director, Clairvest

Leon Raubenheimer, Managing Partner, Zed Financial Partners

Andrew J. Sheiner, Managing Director, Onex Corporation

James B. Walker, Joseph C. Shlesinger, Lawrence N. Stevenson, Managing Directors, Callisto Capital

Stuart D. Waugh, Managing Director, TD Capital Private Equity Investors

M&A Firms and Consultants

Ryan Brain, Partner, Deloitte & Touche LLP

Doug McDonald, Partner, Deloitte & Touche LLP

Robert Palter, Director, McKinsey & Company

Jeff Pocock and Blair Roblin, Partners, Solaris Capital Advisors Inc.

Mark Satov, Satov Consultants Inc. (and his Team)

Jason Sparaga, President, Spara Capital Partners Inc.

Advice and Technical Support

Robert Pouliot, RCP Partners, for conceiving this series and guidance in nurturing it;

Tony Mark, owner, Balance Fitness, who was a source of strength and inspiration;

Mark Shekter and Nancy Trites Botkin, First Star International, for their creative input and consulting;

Ben MacLaren for his patient technical support;

Tom McCullough, CEO, Northwood Stephens Private Counsel Inc., for his referrals to private equity professionals;

Jeff A. Katzin, Vice President and Senior Investment Advisor, BMO Nesbitt Burns, for his help analyzing listed Canadian PE firms.

175

SELECTED READING

Fraser-Sampson, Guy, *Private Equity as an Asset Class* (Chichester, England: John Wiley & Sons Ltd., 2007).

Fraser-Sampson, Guy, *Multi Asset Class Investment* (Chichester, England: John Wiley & Sons Ltd., 2007).

Gladstone, David and Laura Gladstone, *Venture Capital Investing, The Complete Handbook for Investing in Private Businesses for Outstanding Profits* (Upper Saddle River, New Jersey, USA: Pearson Education Inc., FT Prentice Hall, 2004).

INDEX

ABOUT THE AUTHOR

Miriam Varadi spent her career as an investment advisor and ultimately became senior vice president of a major Canadian bank. Her investment practice consisted of high profile Canadians and she ranked as one of the largest asset-managers within the bank's private client division. After a successful 27-year career, Ms. Varadi retired from her practice in 2006 and developed a website for sophisticated investors. Her website articles caught the eye of an editor for Thomson Reuters and she was asked to write this book on private equity.

Ms. Varadi has an in-depth knowledge of investments and has lectured on a wide range of financial topics for professional groups. She has been quoted in various publications.